OUR TRUTH

A Story of Survival

Our Truth-A Story of Survival

Copyright © 2023 by Judi A. Schwab
jaschwab@outlook.com

Library of Congress
Control Number:: 2023905657

ISBN: 979-8-9880757-0-7 (paperback)
ISBN: 979-8-9880757-1-4 (e-book)
ISBN: 979-8-9880757-2-1 (hardcover)

Printed in the USA by Amazon Kindle Direct Publishing. See the back pages of this book for the city and state
where printed.

Cover design and formatting by
 Mandi Lynn-Stone Ridge Books

OUR TRUTH
A Story of Survival

A true story about two sisters who endured years of severe
child abuse, at the hands of their stepfather.

As adults they would become strong survivors, finding peace
and love in the world.

JUDI A. SCHWAB

contributing chapter by her sister
Cherie L. Prater

DISCLAIMERS

My memories are imperfect. The ages, times, events, people, and places noted in this book are to the best of my knowledge and memory. I was a child when I was being abused, and often didn't have "words" for what was happening to me until much later in life. I have written this book using my adult language.

I am not trained in, nor do I have a college degree in any form of social work, including but not limited to psychology or psychiatry.

I have intentionally changed, deleted, or left out a first or last name, or blacked-out names completely if it was essential for privacy, dignity, or legality.

As a forewarning, the subject matter of this book could be traumatizing.

CONTENTS

INTRODUCTION

W e all begin life at a different starting gate. Each of us were born into various family situations: wanted and loved, not wanted, not loved, poor, rich, functional, dysfunctional, no mother or father in the home, no moral guidance, a parent with addiction, mental illness, emotional unavailability, child abuse... too many scenarios to mention. Importantly, our childhood will greatly influence, positively or negatively, the life we lead and what we offer to the world, thus my story. I understand this so deeply because from the ages of five through sixteen years old, I lived in a household where I was abused.

When the parental figures in your life are untrustworthy, uncaring, and don't love you, but inflict injury on you physically, sexually, emotionally, or mentally, as a child you view the world differently and how you interact with others is contaminated by fear and distrust. When you have suffered through deeply traumatic experiences as a young child, it disrupts your nervous system and damages your emotional stability. It instills in you fear and uncertainty. When you are in survival mode at five years old, you are not a child out having fun; you are focused on what might happen next and how to avoid harm, if at all possible. It affects sleeping, eating, learning, caring, loving, trusting, and the desire to thrive and survive. It can affect all the normal stages of your physical, emotional, mental, and sexual development. It changes what you focus on and what you care about. When you are worried about being tortured, raped, or beaten, that spelling test goes way down the list of importance. It changes what matters. It changes how you love. Trust and relationships are difficult, and it carries on into your adult life.

My intention for writing this book is to bring awareness to the fact that child abuse is continuing to happen in our society, and that we must protect our children. We must watch over them with due diligence. The world is full of child abuse victims. It isn't only the creepy guy around the corner we should watch out for. Abuse is commonly committed by someone the child knows, including adults who have authority over and/or access to our children such as family members, teachers, priests, scout leaders, babysitters, neighbors, and friends—or, like my story, the perpetrator lived right in my home: my stepfather. It is crucial to be consciously aware of all adults' involvement in the lives of your children. Teaching children to globally "respect all adults" or "respect your elders" makes them vulnerable to child abuse. I believe we must use our words carefully when we teach our children how to act, speak, or what is expected of them when they are around, or in the care of other adults, or with other children, so we don't remove their voice or power in the situation. Sadly, this includes children that are influential or older than the child. Children do molest and abuse other children. Anyone can be a child molester. **BELIEVE** your children.

I was once told by my counselor that the denial of child abuse occurs more often and is more pervasive than the denial of substance abuse. When we don't believe a child who is being abused, it adds to their victimization.

I want victims of child abuse to know they aren't alone. I want to give a voice to their pain, trauma, shame, and feelings of guilt. Many victims of sexual abuse feel as though they are damaged goods and have some incorrect thought that they have a level of responsibility for what happened. A child isn't ever responsible for any form of child abuse. Tragically, child abuse can be fatal, whether it is by a traumatic injury or suicide. At times, the pain can become unbearable, and suicide appears to be the only way out.

I have known for most of my life that I must share my story to find a greater purpose for the pain and suffering I endured as a child, and the effects of the trauma that I live with as an adult. This story is "OUR TRUTH," and sadly I know it is the truth of millions of other children.

The following is an excerpt from a Christmas Greeting written in 1917 by Grandpa and Grandma Byers, to their **<u>"Dear Children and Children's, Children."</u>** They would be our Great-Great Grandparents. It seemed appropriate to include their guiding words in my memoir. These words were written over a hundred years ago!

*"and...
every one of you
to do your share
to help to make this nation
a place where the poor
and the oppressed
may be protected
and sheltered
and where women
and girls
and sweet and innocent
little children
may happily
and safely
live for all time."*

PART I:

FAMILY DYNAMICS

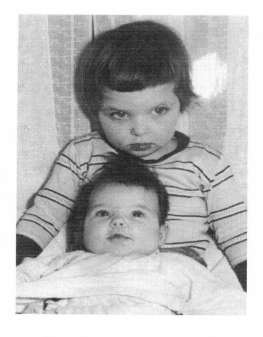

Cherie two-and-one-half years old & Judy three months old

CHAPTER 1

WHERE MY LIFE BEGAN

Birth to Five Years Old

My mother was seven months pregnant with me when my biological parents separated and eventually divorced. Up until then, she and my two-and-a-half-year-old sister, Cherie, had been living in the Florida Keys with our father, David William McNamara. When they separated, Mom and Cherie moved back to Illinois to live with her parents and my aunt, her younger sister Merikay, at their farm in South Grove. My mother resented having to move back home, but she needed help getting her life going again.

A few months later, my mother gave birth to me in a hospital in Sycamore, Illinois without my biological father there to welcome me into the world. I was a healthy nine-pound baby girl she named Judith Annette McNamara. My maternal grandmother, Madge Teresa Defenbaugh-Byers, or "Ole Gram" as she called herself, loved the name Annette and wanted it to be my first name, but she would have to be happy with it being my middle name. I was brought home from the hospital by my mother to join the family and live at my grandparents' farm in South Grove, Illinois for the next few years.

First farm in South Grove, Ill

Grandpa & Grandma Byers in 1932- in their late twenties

Shortly after my birth, my mother returned to work and Ole Gram, or "Gram" as we called her, and Grandpa took care of Cherie and me while our mother worked. Gram was a short, small-framed woman with curly dark hair and a warm, caring heart. Even though she was small, she was strong and powerful when she needed to be. She loved her family and there wasn't anything she wouldn't do for them; she was truly an unselfish soul. Grandpa, Theodore Driscoll Byers, was a big man with broad shoulders and a sensitive nature with a quick wit. Gram and Grandpa didn't have a lot of money, but what they had, they were very willing to share. They believed strongly in families working and being together. They loved us, and we knew it. This was my first experience of unconditional love. I know now how lucky I was to experience this in my most formative years. It gave me the strength to get through what lay on the road ahead of me.

We lived at two different farms during the next five years. The first farm was the larger farm. This was my very first home, in South Grove, Illinois. My grandparents had to sell it at one point, and they then purchased a smaller farm for all of us to live on in Sycamore, Illinois. I was quite young at the first farm and only have a few memories of living there. I do, however, remember bottle feeding the baby owl we found in the barn.

Cherie, Grandpa Byers and Judy

Most of my memories were of the second farm. As young children, it was a sanctuary for Cherie and me. There were animals to play with, rows of corn that surrounded the property, a hammock in the backyard, a pump house, a garden, a chicken coop, a barn, and a small stream that ran through the side of the property. The home was a two-story farmhouse with numerous rooms. The upstairs had two bedrooms with an adjoining walk-through closet that went from bedroom all the way to the other bedroom. It was not only full of clothing but also contained items we liked to play with like "the muff." The muff was a big white furry thing that had an opening through the middle on each side, so you could put your hands into it to keep warm when you went outside on a chilly night in Illinois. It was Aunt Merikay's. Funny the things that stick out in your mind from your childhood. We thought the closet was grand

and played in it all the time. We were happy kids living on the farm. There were many family gatherings and celebrations. We felt the love from our family, and we loved them. Cherie and I had a special bond with our maternal grandparents, Grandpa and Grandma Byers. They were the parental figures in our lives.

Cherie, Aunt Merikay and Judy

Merikay Byers, our mother's younger sister, who was also our grandparents' youngest child and now seventeen years old, was living at home when Mom moved us back to the farm. During those years she helped care for Cherie and me. A few years later, Aunt Merikay would meet a loving and kind man named Cecil Clinton Fletchall, who everyone called "Butch," and he would eventually become her life-long partner and our Uncle Butch when they were married in December of 1963.

Judy & Uncle Butch-December 1963

When they were dating, they would often take Cherie and me along on the date. Aunt Merikay has told me that she and Uncle Butch would feel sorry for us being left at home all the time. They were good to us, had strong family values and loved children. As I write this book, they have been married for fifty-nine years!

Cherie six and Judy four years old-1962

Mom was not a nurturing mother; she was preoccupied with her own needs and wants, and Cherie and I felt that at an early age. I didn't like when she was around and didn't look forward to her coming home. I felt uncertain and uncomfortable around her and saw the unkind way she treated other people and even animals.

Later in life, family members told me that as a child, she resisted the flow of her own family and had difficulty making friends and making good decisions. She could be distant and cruel and didn't want to join in family functions. This was exceedingly difficult for my grandparents as they didn't understand why she acted like this. So now that she was also lacking as a mother, it took a heavy toll on them. They were in their fifties trying to help raise their two young grandchildren, but just like in her early years, she was resistant to their guidance.

Grandpa John, Judy and Cherie

Our paternal grandparents, John and Marie McNamara, lived in the downtown area of Sycamore, Illinois. Occasionally Cherie and I would visit them at their home. Grandma Marie's mother, Great-Grandma Buck, lived with them in the upstairs area of the house. It was set up like an apartment. She had a refrigerator and everything else she needed up there. It was perfect. She had the freedom of living alone, but her daughter and son-in-law were very close by to help if she needed it. I remember going up the lengthy steps to visit her. She was a sweet lady who gave us cold cherry juice out of her refrigerator. She kept it in a tall glass pitcher with a piece of crinkled foil wrapped over the top of the opening. Her apartment was a fun place for us young kids to visit and roam around. She didn't seem to mind but rather enjoyed us being there.

When I was a baby, Grandma Marie took up a new hobby, photography. Cherie and I were her subjects. She even had her own dark room where she would develop the photos she took. Since Cherie and I were her only grandchildren at the time, she took quite a few pictures of us whenever we came to visit.

Judy, Grandma Marie and Cherie

When Cherie was six and I was four years old, Mom began dating a man named Henry Edgar McIntire. She met him at the car dealership where they both were employed. He was divorced and approximately six years younger than Mom. He had two young sons around two and four years old who lived with his ex-wife.

Sometimes we would see Henry for a quick minute when he pulled up in the yard to pick up Mom for a date. He never came into the house or attempted to get to know any of Mom's family, including her mother, father, or her two children. He kept his distance. When Henry drove up, Mom walked outside and jumped in the car, and they were gone. Later that night he would drop her back off, usually while we were sleeping.

Henry and Mom never invited Cherie and me to go on any of their dates, which didn't sit well with the family. Henry didn't attend any family dinners or holiday celebrations with Mom's side of the family, so none of us really got to know him. Uncle Butch was employed by the same car dealership as Henry and didn't like him. Grandpa, who carried a natural intuition about people, didn't have a positive feeling about Henry either. He felt he was sneaky. In less than a year after they started dating, Henry had decided to move out to California and Mom had decided that she wanted to follow him, which she did, leaving us with our grandparents on the farm until she could get settled. She then planned to send for us to come and live with them.

A few months after Mom left Illinois and moved to California to live with Henry, she instructed Grandpa and Gram to put us on a plane and send us out to live with them. Cherie was seven years old, and I was now five years old. Rumor had it that Henry had been running from a child support order for his two sons. At the time, Gram and Grandpa felt that we were Mom's children and that they didn't have a choice but had to follow her request to send us to California. They knew this wouldn't be the best situation for us, yet they couldn't have had any idea how bad the situation would be. I have been told many times that putting us on that plane was the hardest thing our grandparents and aunt and uncle ever had to do. All our eyes were filled with tears as we said goodbye. It would be goodbye for a long time. We were going to be two thousand miles away, too far for them to really know what was going on and too far for us to reach out for help. Too far for anyone to see what our lives would become, what we would have to endure.

My father's parents, Grandpa John and Grandma Marie, were saddened when they found out we would be moving far away, to California. Grandma Marie gave up her photography because she didn't have any interest in it anymore after her "models" were gone.

We were two little girls on their first plane ride to "beautiful" California. During the month prior to leaving, we heard over and over how wonderful California was and how lucky we were to be going there to live. In my five-year-old mind I thought it might be like an amusement park. But even at five years old, I knew I didn't want to leave snowy Illinois, the family I loved and the good life I had there. I could feel everyone trying to build us up to going, maybe they were trying to convince themselves it would be OK. The reality was we were going to live with our mother who didn't take much interest in us and her boyfriend who they really didn't know at all.

I looked over at my older sister, Cherie, sitting next to me and it comforted me that we would share this new life together. Cherie and I had a special bond beyond being siblings. She was my first childhood friend, confidant, and playmate.

Judy four years old, and Cherie six years old, in front of the Christmas tree at Grandpa John & Grandma Marie's home. December 1962

As the plane took off, we unwrapped our gifts and began looking at the new books Grandma Marie and Grandpa John had given us as a going away present to enjoy on the airplane. We had been seated in the front row so we could be cared for by a flight attendant named Gretchen. Later, Aunt Merikay and Uncle Butch would name their first-born daughter "Gretchen," after the flight attendant who watched over us on the long flight to California.

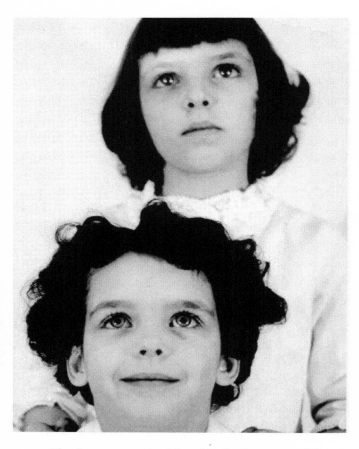

Cherie seven years old and Judy five years old

CHAPTER 2
MOVING TO CALIFORNIA
Five Years Old

After a long flight, we landed in Southern California where it was raining, gloomy, and cloudy. Our Stewardess Gretchen walked us from the plane to Mom and Henry waiting in the airport. When we saw her, there wasn't the excitement and joy you would expect between a mother and the children she'd been away from for two months. She was the same Mom we had had in Illinois, the one who was distant, cold, and focused on her boyfriend Henry.

Once we got to the apartment instead of feeling like a home, it felt sad and lonely. It was small, dark, and quiet. Not at all what I had been used to on the family farm. When Gram and Aunt Merikay packed our suitcase in Illinois, they hid pieces of small wrapped candy all through our clothes. It makes me smile to think about it today. Day after day I would go back to the suitcase and get a piece of candy until one day it was all gone. It felt like the end of my connection to them.

At first when Cherie and I moved into the apartment, Henry was distant and kept to himself. Then over time he would joke around with us, but his jokes had a distorted sense to them, and there would be an underlying cruelty to most everything he did. It didn't take long to see that you couldn't trust him and that he usually had an alternate motive, one that wasn't going to be for the good. When he physically played around with Cherie and me, he quickly became intense and overpowering to the extent that he would hurt us. It would usually end up with Henry physically controlling us by holding our arms behind our backs and tightly squeezing our wrists together so we couldn't get away from him. He would usually make one or both of us cry. I learned early on that it was best to keep my distance from Henry, if possible.

Almost immediately, Henry moved into the role of being the disciplinarian. The first time I remember him "disciplining" me is when I was five years old, and I was trying to execute a gymnastic move on the living room floor. Cherie and I were playing around, and I said the word "butt" while I explained the move. Henry immediately jumped up stating I had said the bad word "butt" and ordering me to go to my room. As I started walking to my room, he kicked me swiftly in the butt and my feet flew up in the air and I dropped to the floor, landing hard on my butt and lower back. As I got up and continued walking to my room, he kicked me in the butt again, and once again my feet left the ground, and I flew up in the air landing painfully on my butt against the floor. In pain, but struggling to move quickly, I tried to get to my room but once again he kicked me in the butt. He did this all the way down the hall until I reached my bedroom. Henry then told me I was grounded as punishment for saying the bad word "butt." This was the beginning of Henry's use of his six-foot-tall, twenty-four-year-old lean body to punish my skinny five-year-old child-sized body. This was also the start of my confusion as to what was right and wrong and why my mother didn't do anything to stop him.

Life in California was hard. Even at five years old, I knew there wasn't any money. Jobs were coming and going, including employment that Cherie and I became a part of, "THE ONION FIELDS." Our entire family would get up early in the morning and drive out to the onion fields to pull onions. The strong aroma and the strength required to pull onion bulbs out of the ground made it an unsuitable task for a five- or eight-year-old child, but Mom and Henry didn't care. They expected Cherie and me to do our share to earn a wage. Plus, this way we were with them, and they didn't need to pay a babysitter. Cherie quietly went along with whatever we were told to do, trying to do her part. I also put effort into it, but it was impossible for me to physically pull the large onion bulbs out of the ground. After a day and a half, it didn't work out, and we didn't report to the onion fields any longer. Mom and Henry were now looking for other ways to make money.

I could feel the tension in the house. They were having financial problems and Cherie and I were two extra burdens. I missed my Gram and Grandpa and our family in Illinois terribly.

I just wanted life to go back to how it was before, when we lived on the farm. I was a scared, lonely little child who ached to be in the loving arms of her Ole Gram. I longed to hear her soft and reassuring voice, telling me everything was going to be OK. But Gram was two thousand miles away.

CHAPTER 3
WETTING THE BED
Six Years Old

In April of 1964, a few months after Cherie and I moved to California, Mom and Henry went to Las Vegas, Nevada to get married. Henry was now our stepfather and Mom told us we were to call him "Dad," so we did. I don't think we had a choice. Seven months later our brother was born. Henry now had a third son and Mom had her third child, but her first and only son. There was now another mouth to feed, and this just added more stress to the already struggling household.

I started wetting my bed in the early hours of the morning while I was sleeping. I was known to be a deep sleeper, but I would be awakened by the warm urine flooding the outside of my pajamas and lower body. Sometimes I would be dreaming that I was on the toilet urinating, but as I became more awake I would realize that I had wet the bed. Fear would immediately race throughout my body because I knew

I was going to suffer horrific punishment. I would just lie in my bed, in the dark, soaking wet and cold, filled with fear of what was going to happen to me once Henry and my mother found out. My mind would race trying to figure out what I could do to change the situation.

Once morning came, I had no choice but to get up and tell them what had happened. Mom would be so angry because she had to wash the bedding and clean up after me. She would state that I was "six years old and too old to be wetting the bed" and then she would ignore me from that point on. They both treated me as though I had done this on purpose. Mom just walked away and stayed away letting Henry do whatever. After all, "I deserved it." Henry would say that he would handle the punishment, and each time I wet the bed, he punished me in many different cruel ways. He was going to get me to quit wetting the bed one way or another.

How could they possibly think I was doing this on purpose? Especially since it resulted in abuse each time. I was a small child; something was obviously wrong. I didn't know how to prevent it from happening, but I would have given anything to be able to stop.

The entire day would be full of his bizarre punishments. I can remember Cherie, between the ages of eight and nine years old, standing next to him as he dealt out the punishment, implying that I was the "bad kid" and she was the "good kid," because she didn't wet the bed. He would ask Cherie what he should do next to me, while I listened from the sideline, feeling scared and hopeless. What an awful and conflicting scenario to teach a child and their sibling. This began a division between Cherie and me.

On the farm in Illinois, we played together and loved each other. Once we were in California, we were pitted against each other by both Henry and Mom. I didn't understand what had happened until I went through counseling in my forties. In-home sexual predators must isolate their victims to protect themselves from being caught. It was intentional and in preparation for future events. Henry was a predator setting the stage. It was better for Henry if we weren't close and confiding in each other. Sadly, he was able to divide us.

Henry taught Cherie she should tell on me when I did something "wrong," that there was a reward to this behavior. She tried to stay on Henry's good side because you knew the severe consequences if you didn't. Henry was able to manipulate Cherie, creating an alliance with her because she was so young and vulnerable. She was his victim just as I was, and none of this was her fault. This alliance tragically broke our close sisterhood. As a young child, I just thought Cherie wasn't nice anymore.

The punishment varied. One punishment was having me pull my pants and underwear down and lie across the bed face down. Then Henry would beat me with the leather belt so hard I would have welts and eventually bruises on my butt and legs, sometimes it would break through the skin and bleed. He used the thin black leather belt that he wore daily. He would unbuckle the belt and pull it out of his pants with a quick jerk, which always scared me to death. As I look back, it probably was his anger rising as he was getting ready to inflict (release?) severe pain upon me. He would then pull his arm back as far as he could behind his back, and with the belt doubled over and held tightly in his hand, he would hit me with full force across my butt and legs. The pain was so intense, my body would cringe, and I would pull my legs up toward the rest of my body. He would yell, "Lay flat!"He would usually tell me ahead of time how many times he was going to hit me with the belt, usually three or four times. It reminds me of things I have seen in movies when people got beatings or strappings. Even though it was only three or four times, it was extremely painful, causing injury to my body. For many days after the punishment, it was painful to walk or sit down.

As another punishment I would have to stand with my head face first against the wall, hands behind my back with my feet and legs spread far apart and away from the wall for hours. My small forehead was bearing the impact of the weight of my body against the wall. Other times I would have to stay in my room for days. I would be made to sleep on the floor without covers, next to my bed. The reasoning here was because I wet the bed I didn't deserve to sleep in my bed. I was cold and wouldn't be able to sleep very well. Later in life, I would learn through my counselor that the punishment I received for wetting the bed was an excuse for Henry to release the rage he carried.

Of course, this didn't stop me from wetting the bed. Sometimes I would wake up as I was urinating. I would run to the bathroom to try and finish going in the toilet, but I had already done "the damage" and the bed was wet. I was in trouble again.

These extreme punishments went on for months until they realized that this wasn't working, and I was taken to the doctor to see if there was a medical problem. The doctor suggested that I not drink any fluids after 6 p.m.. After that was implemented, I didn't wet the bed any longer. Later, as an adult, I learned that a child who wets the bed is often anxious and/or angry.

CHAPTER 4
HENRY BROKE MY LEG
Six Years Old

In the first year of our baby brother's life, he became ill. There were many visits to medical facilities for treatment. On one of the checkups, we all went along but Henry stayed in the car to watch Cherie and me while Mom took our brother inside to see the doctor.

While waiting in the car, Henry started wrestling with us. He was in the front seat of the car but had turned around and was leaning over the back of his seat, taking turns grabbing Cherie or me in the back seat of the car. His "so-called" playful wrestling was straight out physical abuse. It was completely on his terms as to when it started and stopped. He was physically holding, hitting, pushing, twisting, inflicting pain on our bodies and in total control of the situation. He had all the power over us, and he smiled, obviously enjoying it. This was fun for him. We would ask him to stop but he wouldn't, even if we were crying or begging. We were trapped in the back seat of the car and at his mercy.

That day he grabbed my left foot and started twisting it continually in one direction with intense force, making me turn and roll my whole body in that same direction over and over to try and stop the intense pain. I was yelling, "STOP! STOP! PLEASE STOP! OW! OW! OW! OW!!!!" but Henry kept twisting my leg. At one point I couldn't continue to spin my body, but he continued to twist my foot until one of the bones in my leg broke, and everything stopped.

Instantly Henry's face changed. He stopped twisting when he heard the bone break in my leg. He then turned around and sat forward in the car seat. It was as though I hit a wall. I went from spinning, spinning, and spinning, my whole body forced to move quickly to keep myself out of intense pain, to feeling and hearing a snapping noise in my leg, to a complete silence in the car. It took a few seconds to figure out what had just happened, and I then felt fear race intensely through my body. I carefully moved myself back to a sitting position with my legs aligned forward below my body. I don't remember any pain; I must have blocked it out. I looked over at Cherie, who sat to the right of me, next to the car door. She was looking forward in the car with a somber expression. Before long Henry calmly said to me, "When we get home and you go to get out of the car, if you can't walk, I will carry you." From then on, we all sat in the car quietly, no one spoke until our mother and baby brother came back from the doctor appointment. They got into the car, and we all headed home. Nothing was said about my leg.

Once home, we all started to get out of the car, and I immediately knew I couldn't put any weight on my left leg. Henry reached down and scooped me up carrying me into the house. Quickly it was made out that I had "twisted my leg as I got out of the car." Henry laid me on my bed and Mom called the same doctor's office that we had just left, to tell them what had happened...of course it was "their" story...how I had twisted my leg while getting out of the car. After Mom talked to the doctor's office, she told me that we were going to elevate my leg and put ice on it all night. Then in the morning we would return to the doctor's office to get it checked out.

That evening Henry came into my room by himself and reinforced the story of how I broke my leg, "twisting it as I got out of the car when we got home." He gave me a long, disturbing look that sent a deep chill throughout my body and without him speaking any words, I knew exactly what he meant...I was deathly afraid of him, so I wouldn't cross him. After all, he had just BROKEN MY LEG.

Later in life as an adult, Cherie told me that this is the worst memory she has of Henry abusing me. She said she remembers Henry twisting and twisting my leg until it broke and then not telling Mom. During a counseling session when I was an adult, my counselor said that this is very unusual abuse, and that it is cruel and sadistic behavior.

That night, and all night, my leg was elevated in my bed and packed in ice *continuously*, which I doubt was the intention of the doctor. I was freezing. It was a very "cold," lonely night. I lay awake by myself most of the night. Who could sleep with ice packed on your leg all night? There wasn't any "I'm sorry," or any concern. No one came in and checked on me. I lay there fearful about what was to come. Obviously, "I" had only created another burden for our mother.

The next morning Mom and I went to the doctor's office to be treated. I remember hopping around the waiting room because I couldn't put any weight on that leg. Once we were called back, they x-rayed the leg and announced it was broken, one of the bones between the knee and the ankle. Even though I was only six years old, I have a clear memory of the doctor looking down at me and asking me for the second time, "Now, how did this happen again?" The fact that Henry was twisting my leg when this injury happened, most likely would have created a spiral break in the bone. I would later learn that since the early 1980s, spiral fractures of a child's leg or arm are signs of child abuse.

I had no choice but to repeat the same story, the one I was supposed to tell...how I twisted my leg getting out of the car. I was thousands of miles away from the only people I trusted and loved in the world, and I was only six years old. I could see in the doctor's face that he questioned the story, but nothing ever came of it.

The doctor cast my leg from where my toes would join my foot, to the middle of my thigh. It was a very heavy plaster cast, and I couldn't walk or move around by myself. I then went home, where I would be cared for by the same man who broke my leg. I would be wearing the cast on my leg for six weeks.

A few days after Henry broke my leg, Grandma McIntire, Henry's mother, came by for a visit. She boldly walked right into my room, where I had been left lying unhappily on my bed since I was now immobile. She looked at me and with no concern or compassion said, "Ohhh, you are SO clumsy!" making me feel stupid and even more frustrated with the whole situation. I desperately wanted to say, "No! I wasn't clumsy; your abusive son twisted and broke my leg, and then made up this lie to tell everyone. He is a sick and violent man!" but I couldn't. I lay there listening to her demean me, a small child.

I would need crutches to get around, but Mom didn't get them for me. I don't know if it was a money thing or what, but she decided that Henry could just carry me everywhere I needed to go; out to the living room to sit all day, to the bathroom as needed, and to my bed at the end of the evening. Now I was really Henry's victim. There were a lot of times when it was just us and I was completely at his mercy.

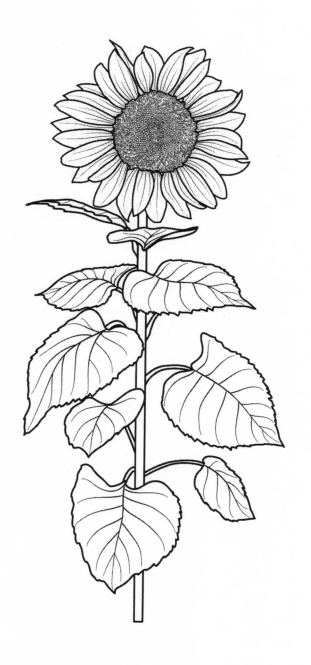

CHAPTER 5
TORTURE, CRUEL AND SADISTIC BEHAVIOR
Six Years Old

After Henry broke my leg and blamed it on my clumsiness, the abuse increased in frequency and intensity. I was terrified of Henry. He could do whatever he wanted to me, and he knew it.

My mother treated me as though she disliked me. It seemed like she didn't care what happened to me, so I couldn't turn to her for help. She always went along with Henry's side of things. I had become the target of their unhappiness and I was subjected to their unwarranted punishment and abuse. I was quickly losing my childhood, my joy, and my interest in life. I felt imprisoned and was always second-guessing my sense of right and wrong. I was full of fear and anxiety, plus my mind was continuously racing, trying to figure out how to keep myself out of trouble, out of danger. Sometimes I existed minute to minute. I had no peace. I could be woken up in the middle of the night and made to get out of bed by Henry for any reason or for no reason. In the daytime, and at any moment, I might be grabbed, hit, punched, or subjected to numerous cruel and painful actions.

I believe my mother was the only one working when I was immobile due to the heavy cast on my leg. Henry was the babysitter for Cherie, me, and our baby brother. I don't remember Cherie being in the room when the abuse was happening. She could have been in school or outside playing with the kids in the apartment complex or she might have gone to bed while I was "lucky" and got to stay up with Henry. I don't remember where our baby brother was either. He must have been in the bedroom in his crib.

Since the heavy cast meant I was immobile, I couldn't even try to stay out of Henry's view. Each day he picked me up out of my bed in the morning and put me in a chair or on the couch in the living room. This is where I stayed during the day. He would carry me to the bathroom and back to the couch or chair as needed, and then to bed at night. There were more opportunities for Henry to abuse me now since I couldn't go to school, and that left time when it was only me and him. One thing about predators, they take advantage of the most opportune times.

The abuse began with Henry coming and sitting right next to my chair in the living room, where I was either watching television or doing my schoolwork. During one of the times, right after he had sat down next to me, I instantly felt a sharp pain on the bottom of my bare foot and I cried, "Ouch!" Henry turned his head, looked at me straight in the eyes, and with a completely blank look on his face said, "What?" acting like he hadn't done anything. He was attempting to conceal what he was doing to me, but I knew he was poking the bottom of my bare foot with something very sharp, like a needle. It wasn't long before our attention went back to the television or homework and then he poked my foot again, and I again yelled, "Ouch!" and he reacted the same way, like he didn't have an idea why I was yelling "ouch." He continued doing this to me a few more times and then he stopped. Decades later, as an adult, I would learn in counseling that this was called "gaslighting." Henry was training me to not trust my own feelings.

On another day he came and sat next to me in the chair. Hiding it from my sight, he held a lighter with the flame lit to the bottom of my foot, while trying to not let me see what he was doing. I felt the hot burn and cried, "OUCH!" and jerked my foot back away from his reach. Then again like his previous denials of not doing anything to me, he would say, "What?" with the same expressionless face. "What are you yelling about, Judy?" He would do it repeatedly, getting the same responses from me and once again answering as though nothing was happening. Then all of a sudden he would stop doing it and walk away. It turns my stomach as I write about this. I was always afraid of what he might do to me next, and I knew I couldn't do anything to stop it from happening.

Henry would try to remove my baby teeth with coins. He would sit next to me and use a nickel or a quarter to try and push or pry my baby teeth out...teeth that weren't loosened yet. I would resist by crying and pleading for him to stop! But he didn't care, and he would just get mad at my resistance and continue to do what he wanted to do. Then at one point he would just get up and walk away.

During the same time period, Henry forced me to eat cigarette butts. Both Henry and Mom smoked, so there were plenty of butts in the house. He brought over the big standalone ashtray, full of them, that he and my mother had previously smoked and sat it next to me in the chair, where I had been put by Henry earlier in the day. Henry told me to open my mouth and then he would forcefully push the butts in my mouth one by one telling me to eat, chew, and swallow them with a very stern voice. They tasted horrible, so I would try to just swallow them, but he would say, "Chew them, chew them up good!" with an angry, threatening voice. He would be inches away from my face as I tried to chew them, while sobbing and choking. You could see the sick humor on his face as I had to succumb to whatever he decided he wanted me to do, and that day it was eat cigarette butts.

If I resisted, it would just increase the abuse. He was going to "win," be "in control," have the "power" over me no matter what. I was very aware of that. Fearfully, I would attempt to both chew the butt and keep it in my mouth without vomiting. I remember the bitter taste of the tobacco together with the dry butt of the cigarette and the burnt, charred remains of the end of the cigarette where it had been burned and then put out, *nasty*. After eating and swallowing a few of those butts, I would begin throwing them up. At this point I would be gagging, vomiting, and crying. You could see in his eyes that he enjoyed the suffering I was going through. There would be a few more days in the near future where I would be forced to eat them again, and of course I would throw up again. The worst part of it all is he would get enjoyment out of doing this to a small, helpless child. Through counseling later in my life, I would learn that this willful cruelty is an indication of a psychopath, or what today is called Antisocial Personality Disorder.

I developed what they thought was pink eye. Rarely were we ever taken to the doctor, so "their" treatment for "pink eye" was putting regular tea that they had brewed themselves in my eye with an eyedropper, and then leaving me in my bedroom with the curtains closed in "a dark room" and having me lie on the bed for what seemed like a week. I don't know exactly how long it was. It felt like forever. One day during this time, Henry came in the room and took my handmade wood guitar that had regular nails pounded in each end of the wood to hold the strings (rubber bands) and began hitting my head with exposed flat tops of the nails. Once again just inflicting pain for his sick enjoyment. He continued hitting me for about five minutes and then he just left the room as usual.

On many separate occasions during this same time period, Henry would bring me into the bathroom and using both of his hands push my head down into a sink filled with water and hold me there with my face submerged, as though he was trying to drown me. I would forcefully try to push my head up against his hands so I could get my face up to breathe, but he was stronger than me and he held my face under the water until I was about to pass out. Then he would let me up out of the water for a few seconds, just so I could barely get a breath and then he would push my head back down into the sink full of water and hold me there with my face submerged again. He would do this numerous times, and then he would just stop. Then at a later date, he would randomly get me and do it again and again. I felt hopeless, scared, and my whole body feared what was in store for me next. I believed Henry was going to kill me either intentionally or unintentionally when he was physically abusing me.

One afternoon Henry forced me to drink straight shots of whiskey. I was once again left at home with Henry to take care of me. He set up shots of whiskey on a small table by my chair and forced me to drink them. The taste was horrible, and I didn't want to, but I didn't have a choice. I don't remember passing out, but I do remember becoming awake and conscious in the bathroom and now it was night-time. Even though my eyes were open, I couldn't see anything except that there was a light on in the room. I could hear my mother's voice saying, "What did you do to her?" and Henry laughing and not admitting to anything, as he held my six-year-old limp body up over the toilet while I vomited and had no control of my physical body. I was so sick, the room was spinning, and I felt like I was going in and out of consciousness with impaired vision. I don't remember how I got to the bathroom or how I got back to bed, or what happened after the bathroom scene. When I think of this story, I have hatred for Henry, but I have even more hatred for my mother. How could she let this happen to me? How could she be with this man? She shared a life and home with him in the daytime and then she crawled in bed with my abuser at night. How did she live with herself? How did she get up in the morning and look in the mirror? I thought mothers were supposed to have a strong instinct to protect their children.

I didn't have anyone around me I trusted to go to for help. I didn't have trust in my mother. She confirmed my suspicions that I couldn't trust her by not doing anything to protect me the night she came home and found me intoxicated in the bathroom with Henry, after he had forced me to drink the whiskey. Nothing changed after that day. Mom never said anything to me about what had happened, and she didn't question me on a later date, when I was sober. But she did continue to leave me alone in Henry's care. I'm sure that each time Henry was able to abuse me without consequence, it just validated his power and control over me.

I wanted to be able to reach out to Gram and Grandpa, or other family for help, but they were two thousand miles away in Illinois. At six years old, I didn't have any idea how to call or write to them without Henry or Mom knowing. I didn't even have their phone number or know how to dial the phone. I hadn't ever called anyone by myself. I didn't know how to mail them a letter. I didn't have their address or know how to write it on an envelope, or how to get postage. I was in the first grade. I could barely write! How could I express in words what was happening to me while I lived in California?

Cherie was eight years old, and we weren't close any longer. Henry had destroyed that bond. Since she had been taught to tell on me by Henry, that is probably what would have happened if

I had asked her if she could help me contact our grandparents. I didn't know how to stop what was happening to me. I didn't trust anyone at my school. They were all adults who were in charge, and I just did what they told me to do, or I got in trouble.

Henry had instilled so much fear in me through pain and suffering that I was afraid to cross him. Even if I were able to contact them, I don't believe they could have understood how dangerous it could have been, had they brought this out in the open while leaving me in the home under Henry's care. Mom would have supported Henry and maybe even lied for him. I would have again been made out to be the "bad kid" who didn't want to follow the rules. In denial or in a neglectful way she had already helped Henry cover up the truth about my broken leg. She never asked me directly what happened.

Henry always told us that he was our parent, and that he could do anything he wanted to do to us. I believed him, he was doing everything and anything that he wanted to do to me, and no one was stopping him. He was right.

CHAPTER 6
SEXUAL ABUSE—RAPE OF A CHILD
Beginning at Six Years Old

This is the most difficult chapter to write, but also a very crucial one. I believe putting it down on paper is giving it to the universe for any and all benefit that it could serve to help others.

The sexual abuse started when I was about six years old. It happened over and over too many times to count. It could happen weekly, a few times a week or a few times a month. It depended upon the opportunity Henry had to get Cherie and/or me alone at home without Mom being there. I lived in fear on a daily basis that at any time the opportunity for one of us to be left at home with him could easily happen, especially since Mom wasn't the nurturing type who wanted us with her. She usually did what was best for her, which was leave us at home.

I was a typical thin to average-sized young child. My very first memory of the sexual abuse was at an apartment in San Jacinto, California. Mom wasn't home and I'm not sure where Cherie or my baby brother were at the time. The memory of this incident is very vague, but I can still visualize myself laying naked from the waist down, in a darkened room, on Mom and Henry's bed, and being touched in the genital area by Henry.

The next memory of sexual assault is a few months later at an older yellow rental house that we had moved into in Valle Vista, California. It was secluded and the backyard was fenced, dividing it from the surrounding fields and rolling hills. Our younger sister had just been born, so there were now four siblings. Cherie was nine years old; I was seven years old, and our younger brother was just turning a year.

My mother and Cherie weren't home at the time. I was told by my stepfather Henry to go into his bedroom and take off my pants and underwear and then lie face up on their bed. He then came into the room and positioned how he wanted me on the bed. He swiftly opened the front of his jeans and immediately laid on top of me. He never let me see him with his pants open or his genital area, he would move quickly and keep himself covered. He never took his clothes off, he just unbuttoned and pulled open his pants as he lay on me. I could feel the buttons of his jeans as they were painfully being pushed into my naked body. I immediately felt crushed by his body weight on top of me and I was unable to breathe very well. He started moving his body, pushing down on me. I immediately felt an excruciating sharp pain in my genital area. The pain was so extreme and unbearable.

I had no idea what he was actually doing to me. At seven years old I didn't have any in-depth knowledge of the male anatomy and I couldn't visibly see what he was doing. I had no idea I had a vagina. As a young child, all I could imagine is that he was scratching or cutting my genital "private" area with his fingernails or something else that was very sharp and creating horrible pain. I felt like I was being tortured and torn apart in the genital area. It felt like he was sticking a knife down there. I was screaming and crying stop! Please stop! Over and over with the little breath I had as the weight of his body on my chest continued to make it hard to breathe. He continued, my painful cries to stop didn't seem to have any effect on him. I kept crying and asking him to stop, begging him to let me go to the bathroom. At one point he let me get up and I ran into the bathroom and sat on the toilet trying to escape from the horrible pain and torture. My genital area was throbbing with pain. I stayed there as long as I could, but he told me to hurry up and that I had to go back and lie on the bed again, as I was before. I fearfully returned and he lay back down on me and continued to painfully violate my small body. Again, all I could feel was the most horrible pain and being crushed and unable to breathe. I was trying to keep my focus on making it through this violent act and the excruciating pain. At the end of the assault, I felt a wet sensation in my genital area, and he stopped moving. Henry then got off me, putting his pants back together quickly where I couldn't see what he was doing.

When I was older and understood what having sex and sexual relations meant, I pieced together what he had done to me. He was raping me until he orgasmed and the sharp pain I was feeling was him tearing me apart as he penetrated my vagina.

When Henry was done, he told me to stay on the bed as I was, and he used some type of an antiseptic cleanser on my genital area. It seemed like he had done this before. I guess he didn't want me to get an infection because that could possibly cause him to get caught. He then let me go into the bathroom and told me to clean up and get dressed.

I sat on the toilet feeling my whole genital area burn and throb and it continued to hurt for days after each rape, especially when I needed to use the restroom. I was a little girl who had no idea what had just happened to her. What I did know is that something was very wrong. I was now even *more* afraid of Henry.

I washed up, got dressed, and went out to the living room where he was watching television. Henry then threatened me. He said if I told anyone I would be in deep trouble. I knew that meant that if I told anyone he would inflict severe pain on me. He would then give me some money, usually a dime or a nickel; sick. I was terrified of Henry, and he knew it. I felt unvalued, unloved, and unimportant. I felt like nothing. I felt trapped, captured in a situation I had no power to get out of. I didn't feel free.

At seven years old, I didn't know how to get help or change the situation. If I had a mother who cared, it would have been different. I could have gone to her. Henry's actions would leave blood stains on my underwear. That underwear went into the hamper for my mother to wash. Why wouldn't a mother wonder what blood was doing on her seven-year-old daughter's underwear?

During this time, Henry worked in the rose fields. After work he would come home with the strong stench of rose bushes on his body and his clothing. His job entailed tying the rose branches up in a particular way, using thin strips of stretchy rubber that in the end, would stimulate the plant to produce more roses. To help him complete his duties he had a metal cart with bicycle wheels and a beige fabric covering for the sides and top that would shade him. He kneeled on the ground and leaned into the cart, rolling it along each row of the large field, as he tied up every rose bush. I remember the awful smell on his hands after work where he would grab me and hold me tight, forcing his fingers down my throat to make me gag. Years later in counseling I learned that sometimes that is done to prepare the victim for oral sex, a sadistic grooming process.

It wasn't long before I realized that my older sister, Cherie, was also being sexually abused by Henry. He waited until my mother left the house and for a while it was every Friday, when our mother went to the grocery store for about an hour to do the weekly shopping. He would lock up the house and rape either Cherie or me during the time she was gone. The one who was raped that day depended upon who Mom wanted to take with her to help with the grocery shopping. The daughter left behind, got raped. Another horrific part of this is that our one-year-old brother and infant sister were also at home, left under Henry's care.

Mom would be getting herself ready to go shopping, and Cherie and I would each beg her to go along. If Cherie were chosen to go shopping, I would always start crying extremely hard. I was in complete fear of what was to come and couldn't stop crying even though I knew it was going to make things worse for me. Henry would angrily tell me to go to my bedroom because I was crying. Mom and Cherie would then leave to go grocery shopping. Henry would quickly lock up the house and then come into my bedroom and start punching me in the stomach, beating me up because I was crying, telling me, "STOP CRYING! SHUT UP AND STOP CRYING NOW! OR DO YOU WANT MORE?"

Now I would be lying on my bed and gasping for breath because he punched the air out of me. He would then leave my room for a brief time for me to "straighten up" (his words) and then he would come back in and tell me to go into his bedroom and take off my pants and underwear and lie on his bed. Then the same thing would happen as before. He would lay on me and violently rape me. After it was over, I would return to the living room where he was watching television and as usual, he would threaten me to not tell anyone! Again, he would usually give me one or two coins so I could buy some candy. It sickens me to think back on all of this. I think of that little child. So awful. Many years later, in counseling Cherie told me that he didn't beat her up like he did me. Our counselor said that by crying I was displaying the damage that the perpetrator was doing, and he didn't want to see that. So he beat me up to shut me up, as if my crying would break through his veil of denial, causing him for a moment to see his cruel sadistic nature.

46

When Cherie had to stay home with Henry she didn't cry or show any emotion. She knew it wouldn't help and thought it might not be as bad if she didn't fight him. Her way of handling it was nonresistance; to do what he said and just get it over with. She said Henry would sexually assault her the same way he assaulted me. Our counselor asked Cherie how she coped with the sexual assault, and she said she just closed her mind, she just held it inside. Our counselor asked, "What does it mean to close your mind?" Cherie said, "I don't think about what is happening, I just exist there and let it happen." Both Cherie and I agree that immediately after being sexually assaulted we felt this weird sense of relief, because we knew we could live for a short while without the fear of being raped at any moment. I never knew why, but there were always days in between each sexual assault.

While Cherie was at home being sexually assaulted by Henry, I was at the store thinking about Cherie left behind, going through the sexual assault and pain. When we got home, I remember watching Cherie's face to see how she was doing. It was heart-wrenching knowing he had just raped her, yet everything just went along as though all was normal.

There came a time where Henry wasn't working, and Mom was. He was now at home every day to take care of us. Cherie and I didn't always ride the same bus home from school because of our age/grade difference, so at times there would be an opportunity for Henry to sexually assault whoever got home first. As Cherie said, "you didn't know whether to walk home slowly from the bus stop or to go quicker and just get it over with." If Mom weren't home but both Cherie and I were home, sometimes he would still be willing to rape Cherie. I'm not sure why he made that decision. Our counselor said it was probably because of the lack of resistance from Cherie. Henry could maintain his delusion of doing nothing wrong, or that she might even like it.

I have some very traumatic memories of Cherie being told to come inside the house and me being told to stay outside of the house. Once Cherie went in, I then heard Henry walk through the house locking all the doors and closing all the windows. As I sat on the back-door steps of the house, I would hear Cherie's piercing screams and her uncontrollable crying as he brutally raped her. She would yell, "NO, NO, NO!" Even though Cherie tried to take the approach of nonresistance, the extreme pain she suffered while being raped overtook her ability to be compliantly silent.

Hearing Cherie's painful cries was very traumatizing for me. I still react both physically and emotionally to this memory today when I hear a child crying and I can't physically see them to know what is making them cry. I mentioned this in counseling and our counselor suggested to let myself sit with the crying, to experience the feelings and emotions associated with the memory of pain, anger, fear, and helplessness. Our counselor said I should validate my feelings about this awful experience, that it would be normal to react the way I do. He said, "These are post-traumatic reactions." I have followed my counselor's advice and shed many tears trying to work through it.

One day Mom took all of us kids to town when she had some shopping to do. She left us in the car while she went into the store. She had informed us that she was going to go into one store and then she would come out and go into another store, while we were waiting for her. I noticed that Cherie was in deep thought, staring straight ahead as she sat quietly in the front passenger seat. When we saw Mom come out of the first store Cherie said, "Wait here, I am going to go talk with Mom." I watched as Cherie walked up to Mom and they talked, standing outside of the store. I saw the seriousness in Cherie's face, and I just knew deep inside that she was telling Mom that Henry was sexually assaulting "us." I thought Cherie was very brave, but I was also afraid for her that day. I was hopeful that this was going to make a desperately needed change in our lives. They came back to the car, and you could sense the tension, plus neither said a word as Mom drove home.

One would assume that when Cherie stated that she was being sexually abused by Henry, thoughts of the younger, eight-year-old daughter Judy crying intensely every time she was left home alone with Henry, or the random blood found in her underwear, would have formed a question in our mother's mind. It probably did, but she never asked me. I do not think she cared if it was happening to me or not. This was how she typically treated me. I was not important. I was only a burden. I don't think she would have protected me if I had told her. Later in life she would validate my suspicions.

As a child who lives with an abuser, you become hypervigilant to what is going on in the household. You carefully observe the emotional tone and all the interaction with the other members of the family. This awareness helps to keep you safe and alert, so you don't add additional stress to a volatile situation. That being said, there were many quiet conversations between Henry and Mom later that day. I believe Mom told Henry that Cherie said he was sexually abusing her.

Mom knew deep inside what Cherie told her was the truth. She knew she would have gotten the same answer from me. She didn't want to have to admit to the world what her husband was, or that her marriage was a facade. Even though Mom indicated she didn't believe Cherie, Mom also didn't leave Cherie home alone with Henry any longer. But Mom did continue to leave me home alone with him. The sexual abuse stopped for Cherie, which I am so grateful for, but it continued for me, increasing in frequency.

There were days where Mom was gone from the house because she started working on the weekends. Henry would be at home, in the house taking care of our younger siblings, who were babies. Cherie would be able to leave and go to a friend's house, but I would be left at home with Henry. I would quickly go outside and wander the yard, praying Henry would forget about me. I never wanted to go into the house to use the restroom because I thought it might trigger him. But sometimes I would have to because I couldn't wait any longer. I would quietly open the back-screen door, sneak into the bathroom, and then sneak back out again. The television was always on and usually loud, it helped me to get in and out unnoticed. Having lunch, snacks, or drinks on those days was out of the question. It was too risky to have any contact with Henry. We had fruit trees in the yard, and if they were in season I would eat off them. I had also located a large gunny sack of walnuts in a small shed on the property and I would go and eat some of those on days that I was outside and hungry. I would get a drink of water out of the hose. Most of those days I was too nervous to eat. I was riddled with the fear of suffering severe pain that I couldn't do anything about. It is all I could think about.

I would find a spot in the yard that was out of sight where I could sit alone with my arms wrapped tightly around my legs holding them close to my chest, with my face buried down on my knees, whimpering over the pain and suffering I had already been subjected to by Henry, and knowing that today I might have to endure it once again. I never wanted my mother around, she was cruel and hateful to me, but in these circumstances, I needed her around. My mother's presence in the house is what protected me from being sexually abused by Henry. Not anything that she did or said, just her presence.

After Mom was gone for a while, I would have hope that she would come home soon, so I would sit in the dirt by the corner of the fence and watch the highway for Mom's car to appear around the corner. When I saw it, I knew she would be home within minutes and the possibility of being raped by Henry that day was over. But there were also days where Henry would come outside early in the day to look for me. When he found me he would make me go back into the house with him, where he would sexually assault me the same way he had before.

The violent sexual assaults continued for the next few years. For brief moments during an assault, I was learning to dissociate physically, mentally, and emotionally; separating my consciousness from my experience. It meant that during those moments, I was no longer experiencing what my body was experiencing. I was a child trying to hold on and make it to the other side of every assault, and it was becoming extremely difficult. I had no voice or value. I existed only to serve Henry's needs. The anxiety became overwhelming, I was on the edge of an emotional breakdown. I was suffering deeply, I just wanted to die. It would be easier. I could just go away forever and not have to experience this anymore.

Henry continued raping me until I was about ten years old, then it stopped. There was another sexual assault when I was eleven to twelve years old. Our family was swimming over at our friend's house and numerous times Henry put his hands in my bathing suit bottoms and fondled me while we were in the pool. He was always destroying any joy in my life. The physical, emotional, and mental abuse continued, and I lived with the fear that at any time he would start sexually abusing me again.

Throughout our entire childhood, Cherie and I never had a conversation about what Henry was doing to either one of us. Cherie kept to herself and went about life her own way. I didn't trust Cherie and that was just as Henry intended for our relationship to be. It kept his secrets of abusing each of us hidden much longer.

When I was in my late teens, I tried to bring up the subject to Cherie a few different times, but to no avail. She would just end the conversation or walk away. I quit trying and left it alone. I was confused about it all, but I also realized that it wasn't a subject that she was going to talk about.

Being sexually assaulted as a child never leaves you. It is so important for family and friends to understand this, and to validate the individual who has suffered being subjected to this horrific crime. You don't just get over it and move on. It happened to You, and it is Your Truth. I want to validate every child abuse victim. It doesn't define you, but it is a part of who you are. All of us are everything we have ever experienced, both positive and negative.

Standing in the truth of who you really are doesn't make you a victim. It is an admirable act of being your authentic self, which in turn can help you to heal and be the best and most beautiful You.

Judy nine years old and Cherie eleven years old

CHAPTER 7
GRANDMA MCINTIRE
Henry's Mother

Myrtle Mae McIntire, Henry's mother, was a short and stout woman who had long white hair with a yellow cast. Her hair was so long that it hung below her buttocks when she would let it down to comb it out. She always wore her hair up on top of her head by parting it in the middle, making it into two long braids and bobby pinning the braids back and forth across the top of her head. She was from the south, with a strong southern accent and a tough exterior.

Grandma McIntire, as we called her, never learned to drive a car, but walked everywhere she needed or wanted to go, even as she aged. She usually wore a straight, sleeveless dress, "a shift," with the length hanging somewhere between her knees and ankles. She never, ever wore pants. She also wore a man's long-sleeved dress-shirt over her dress, in order to protect her arms from the sun. Some days she would just show up at our home, which meant that she walked clear across town on a hot day to get there, without calling to see if someone could come and pick her up. She was a strong and independent woman.

It seems important for me to include what I knew about Grandma McIntire because she was Henry's mother. I always wondered what influence or effect, if any, she or his father, had on the man he became, who was cold, violent, and horrifically abused children.

Grandma McIntire had four biological children that I knew of, but over the years I heard through family discussions, that she had many more children. I'm not sure what that meant or where they were. She was poor and lived a very tough life, her children had to work in the cotton fields at a young age, picking cotton to help support the family. I was told that she lived most of her life in Oklahoma and Texas, but when I met her she lived alone in Southern California. She wasn't married at the time and never had a significant other in her life during the time I knew her.

She was a religious woman and gave a lot of her time and the little bit of money she had to the church. She was always baking pies for the minister or doing whatever else she could do to help him personally, or to help down at her church.

When she was home, she would switch the television channels between watching the Roller Derby or the evangelists. Her faith was very important to her, but she also loved the Roller Derby, and you couldn't tell her that any of the fighting or dramatic acts weren't real, she believed it all. She definitely had her favorite skaters and would get vocally excited or angry as she watched it.

Grandma McIntire made all different sizes and colors of quilts and also sewed clothing. She would make special quilts or clothing for her biological grandchildren, two of them were our younger siblings, but never for Cherie or me. I guess because we weren't her "blood," she couldn't find the love or desire to do something kind for her step-grandchildren. She would come to the house with her homemade gifts for our younger siblings, giving the gifts to them right in front of Cherie and me. She acted very self-righteous about it, showing no remorse that she didn't have something for all of the children in the house.

She would occasionally babysit the four of us, sometimes for a weekend. It was during those visits that she would say unkind things to Cherie and me. She would tell us that she didn't like our mother, and then she would say, "You know that you two aren't H.E.'s kids!" She would call him by his initials, "H.E.," short for Henry Edgar, his first and middle name. It made me feel like we did something wrong by simply being who we were. It was once again that feeling of "lesser than" when I was in her presence.

Grandma McIntire had so many habits that were different than what we were used to. When it was time to clean her teeth, she would go right outside and get a stick off a particular bush or tree. It had to be chosen correctly because it needed to be soft enough to spread open on the end like a brush. She knew exactly which bushes or trees had the right sticks. She also told us that she would use a leaf from a bush to clean herself prior to having toilet paper. She had many stories and as kids we were very interested in them or freaked out by them! The stories sounded like they came right out of the old west...from the 1800s.

She had lots of sayings that I hadn't ever heard before like "he was so dumb he couldn't pour piss out of a boot!" spoken with a southern accent. She chewed snuff and spit it into a tin can that she had taken from our trash and then torn off the outside label. Then she would save her "spit can," leaving it at our home down in a cupboard so that she could use it the next time she came over. Of course, my mother wouldn't want that "dirty" can under the cupboard in our kitchen, so she would throw it away. The next time Grandma McIntire came over and couldn't find her spit-can, it would make her so mad. But she would just make up another one and leave it under the cupboard once again.

If she went in the car with us and her spit-can wasn't under the seat of the car where she had left it the last time she rode with us, she would spit her snuff right out the window, which would get all down the side of the car! That would make my mother so angry, especially because she was excessively clean when it came to her house or her car. It seems like they were constantly having a passive-aggressive battle. They obviously didn't like each other.

She wasn't a nurturing grandma, but she could make a mean pot of pinto beans that you ate along with her cornbread or homemade biscuits. I loved watching her make those biscuits, it was magical how she could quickly make them up into perfectly shaped biscuits using one hand. Then she would dip them in melted butter before she put them in the oven. She was known for a relish that she made by hand called "chow-chow." Her own special recipe, it was made with green (unripe) tomatoes. I was taught to eat it with the pinto beans. It was really good.

There was another side to Grandma McIntire that I didn't trust. It seemed like she always tried to throw us under the bus when she was babysitting us. When our mother and Henry would come home and ask how we were while they were gone, she would often complain to them (as she chuckled) that Cherie or I did something too slowly or not perfectly. If Henry thought we were giving his mother any trouble while we were in her care, there would be a big price to pay.

Henry was completely respectful to his mother, and she was the same way to him. He wouldn't let anyone harm her and would help her if she wanted or needed something. But I also saw that there were boundaries that she didn't cross when she was around him or spoke to him. She was careful about her words, and if she said something that he didn't like, he was quick to stop her in her tracks, and she did stop. There weren't ever any arguments or cross words between her and Henry. As far as Grandma McIntire was concerned, her adult children were the best, they were shining stars and she strongly protected them. They could do no wrong. If there were any problems in the household, it would be their wife's or children's fault because they were *"perfect sons."*

Grandma McIntire passed away many years ago, in the late seventies, when I was a young adult.

CHAPTER 8

LIFE AT THE OLD YELLOW RENTAL HOUSE

Seven to Nine Years Old

O nce the two younger siblings were born, Henry usually worked full-time, and Mom was employed off and on at a few different part-time jobs. She worked at fast food restaurants so she could work when Henry wasn't working, like nights and weekends. He would then be the one at home to watch us kids. These jobs came and went for Mom, she never worked consistently. I know she needed the income it could provide, but I was always glad when she didn't have a job. When she was home, Henry didn't sexually abuse us.

Henry and Mom would occasionally go to Las Vegas together for the weekend. During that time, Grandma McIntire would come stay at the house, and take care of us four kids. Since she was Henry's mother, we knew that we better be on our best behavior, or we would be in trouble with Henry. She wasn't going to take any "guff" from us kids, especially not Mom's children. If we were "misbehaving," she would make the older kids go and pick their own switch off the "switch tree," while threatening that they better straighten up or she was going to whip them with it. Spending time with Grandma McIntire could be challenging, but it was much better than being with Mom and Henry. It created a short mental and physical break for us.

As soon as Henry and Mom felt Cherie was old enough to babysit, they left us in her care. She was probably ten to eleven years old when she was in charge of caring for us three kids. Since our siblings were quite young, Cherie would focus on caring for the youngest child, our younger sister, and I would focus on caring for our younger brother. I was about eight years old at that time. Mom and Henry gave us strict rules to follow when they were going to be gone for the weekend. We all had to stay in the house, and we couldn't answer the door if someone came knocking. Cherie was in charge of answering the phone and had specific instructions on what to do, depending on who was calling. Luckily, everything always went well, and there weren't any mishaps. That was greatly in part because Cherie was mature and obedient at a young age; she always followed the rules. We were growing up quickly.

Henry stopped sexually abusing Cherie after she told Mom what was happening, but he was still sexually, physically, mentally, and emotionally abusing me. Mom was also emotionally and mentally abusing me. Often one child is targeted in a family where there is abuse, and I had become that child. It was so difficult to live and function in that environment. The abuse affected every part of my life. It was challenging to focus on school and to learn what I was being taught. Or to simply enjoy playing. The abuse I had suffered and the possibility of being abused at any time was always on my mind. I often didn't feel well. Most days I was nervous and guarded, worrying that something violent and painful could suddenly happen to me. I lived a continual lie and was required to tell lies because I couldn't tell the truth of what was really happening at home. But at the same time, I was held to a strict order of not telling any "other" lies, or I would be punished for it. I was so confused about how to act and speak, and how I was supposed to behave or feel. It changed me. My emotional response was affected, and I no longer responded correctly to a variety of situations. It was changing my brain.

Henry's two young biological son's came to live with us for a couple of months. I believe the oldest son was six years old, and the younger son was four years old. There were some child custody and support issues going on between Henry and the boy's mother. She had stopped by our house a few times and they seemed like random events, like maybe she finally found out where Henry lived. Henry and Mom would quickly go outside and meet her and her significant other outside of their car in the far end of the front yard and talk. I couldn't hear what they were saying. They weren't ever allowed in the house. These meetings didn't look warm and friendly either. Before long, Henry's two sons were dropped off to live with us. There were now six children to feed and care for in the house.

Henry turned our screened-in porch into a bedroom for his two older sons. Mom was cold and mean to them, she wanted them gone. She was cruel to her own daughter, her own flesh and blood, so you can imagine how she was to these two young boys. I felt sorry for them, I was feeling the same pain and suffering as they were living in a house where you weren't wanted. I remember the youngest boy crying a lot. Henry never showed much parental interest in them or any of his children. Neither Mom nor Henry were nurturing or compassionate parents. It was more like they were doing what they had to do: feed, shelter, clothe, and send us to school. The boys left with their mother one day and never returned. I don't know where they are or what happened to them. I never saw them again or heard their names mentioned. Life just went on. Those boys were much better off without Henry in their lives.

Mom continually confirmed that she had no interest in protecting me or my safety. I would be sent to the Valle Vista Store on my bicycle, a mile one way, uphill on the main highway. Their car was often sitting in the garage. She or Henry just didn't want to get up and go to the store themselves. Sometimes it would be early Saturday morning because she wanted to cook breakfast and needed some ingredients. It was cold out and she wanted me to hurry up and get back. I didn't have a basket on my bike, so I had to be able to hold the food and ride my bike back home. If I got home and I didn't have the correct change from what I had spent, she would make me ride my bike all the way back to the store to get the difference that was owed to her. It was always under a dollar, just some change. It could be twenty cents, and I would be made to go back and get it.

Household chores that were assigned to me during these years were often unreasonable and beyond the ability for someone my age. I was expected to do these chores perfectly, and if I didn't (couldn't), then I wasn't doing what I was told to do. I was misbehaving and would get punished for it. I was continuously being set up to fail. There wasn't a learning period for anything. You were told to do it, and you better do it well. I would have to wash the dishes by hand when I was about seven to eight years old. To do this I had to stand up on a box so I could reach the sink. This was a big job for an eight-year-old, especially to do it well. If I failed to get one dish clean, I would have to wash all the dishes, including the pots and pans all over again. That happened quite often. Henry would look at the clean dishes and pans that were piled up in the drainer until he found one that had something on it and that would be it! I had to rewash everything again. I tried awfully hard to do the best job I could, but I was overwhelmed.

One day while I was washing the dishes in the kitchen, I missed seeing my younger brother, who was about eighteen months old, get into a cupboard behind me and pour dry powder soap out on the floor. When Henry came into the kitchen and saw this, he began yelling at me for not watching him and punched me in the face with a closed fist. The punch launched my whole body straight back into the refrigerator behind me, where I hit the back of my head and fell to the floor. I immediately had a bloody nose and I think that I went unconscious for a few seconds. He possibly broke my nose that day. There were no doctor visits, we cleaned it up and moved on. I "deserved it" because I wasn't watching my younger sibling. Later in life I would learn from my counselor that child abuse victims often begin to believe they deserve the abuse they are suffering, by "buying into the punishment cover-up."

I was told on a regular basis by Mom or Henry that I was either doing something wrong or saying something wrong, or I looked at them wrong, or that somehow everything was my fault. I was always failing at everything as far as they were concerned. This greatly affected my sense of self. I wasn't treated the same as the other siblings. One day when Cherie and I brought our report cards home, Cherie had made an improvement in one of her grades. I saw Mom rewarding her with a little bit of money. I had always gotten good grades and didn't get rewarded, so I mentioned this to Mom. She just said, "Oh, it's easier for you to get good grades than Cherie," and that was that. I didn't get any money that day for my good grades.

In September of 1966 Grandpa Byers offered to pay for the gasoline if Henry and Mom would drive our family back to Illinois so they could meet their new grandson and granddaughter. They agreed to make the trip. Cherie was now ten years old, and I was a month away from being eight years old. Our younger brother was almost two years old, and our younger sister was almost a year old. Mom was happy that her parents were going to meet the two new grandchildren for the first time. I was thrilled that we were going. I missed my grandparents and family in Illinois terribly. But the trip was very short, a week in total, including the driving time. We had about three days to visit with everyone.

Once we arrived in Illinois and I smiled at Gram, she could see I wasn't getting any dental care while I was living in California.

Both of my top front teeth were black, so she took me to the dentist and my grandparents paid for these teeth to be removed. I remember the discussion among the adults about why my teeth were black; I probably ate too much candy. But now I wonder if there was a different reason. Those teeth weren't full of cavities, and they were firm in place and no decay. I would now question if the reason they were black is because the nerves were dead in those two teeth, possibly from the day when Henry punched me in the face, or other times that he had physically abused me.

As usual, Mom just went along with Henry and whatever he wanted while we were visiting in Illinois. She acted as though everything was wonderful and going great out in California. She wasn't going to admit that she made a bad decision and was in a bad marriage again. By being two thousand miles away she could tell any story she wanted to about her life in California. She was good at putting on the airs, and that is what she did.

Cherie, Aunt Merikay, Judy in Illinois- 1966

I loved being back with my family on the farm, but at the same time, I felt Henry's heavy presence always nearby. For a fleeting moment I was safe and back with my grandparents where I longed to be, but I couldn't stay. It created immense turmoil inside of me. I could not tell them that Henry was abusing us, how he had raped me and Cherie, and broken my leg, because I was so fearful of Henry. I was weak, broken, and unable to speak my truth. I was an invisibly controlled and silenced victim.

What if I was able to tell and they confronted Henry, but we were still sent home to California. I knew that was a big possibility and I couldn't risk it. He would have been so angry. I am sure he would have made me suffer because of it. I was too young and afraid to fight this battle. Henry had tortured, suppressed, and conditioned me to believe he was in control since I was five years old. Mom had enabled all of his horrific behavior and he could continue this abuse because she allowed it. We were in a different state for a few days, but she wasn't in a different state of mind. She was my biological mother and had full custody of me. He was her husband, and she wanted their marriage to continue. She wanted to be his wife...or maybe just a wife? This was the time to step up if she wanted to get us out of this abusive situation, to save her children. But she didn't do anything to help us. I knew what I had experienced from Henry, and at that time in my life he WAS the final word. My everyday existence was living that finality of abuse and pain.

It was extremely difficult for me to leave Illinois at the end of the visit, but I didn't have a choice. I cried all the way home with my head buried in the back seat of the car, trying to hide my emotions. I feared that Henry or Mom would get mad at me for being emotional, because I wasn't allowed to cry at home. It was heart-wrenchingly painful as I was being driven away from the safety of my grandparents.

Back home in Southern California, I made friends with a girl my age who lived in the neighborhood. We met because she went to the same school bus stop as I did. Occasionally, I was able to go over to her house and play. She was a really nice girl and we had fun spending time together. One day she shared with me that on Saturdays her father had a side job installing flooring in trailers. He would take her with him to the side job, and during the time they were there, he would make her perform oral sex on him in the trailer until he ejaculated. I was shocked and horrified by this, but also alarmed by the fact that another girl my age was also being sexually abused. Was this happening everywhere? I never told her what we were going through with Henry. I was always too afraid that it might come back to him and that he would do something even more horrible to me than he already had. From that day forward, I was scared to death of her father, and never wanted to be in the same room with him when I was over at their home. Years later she moved to another state and sadly I don't know what happened to her.

Grandma Marie and Grandpa John tried to stay in touch with us after we moved to California. They wrote letters and sent gifts on birthdays and holidays, plus they came out to visit us a few times over the years. They would come and stay in a hotel in the area. During their visits, they weren't ever allowed in our home. They would come and pick us up then drop us back off. You could feel the tension between them and Mom. She didn't make it easy on them. I can remember Mom saying, "What do I need to do?! Roll out the red carpet for them to come and visit their grandchildren?!"

When I was nine years old and Cherie was eleven years old, Grandma Marie and Grandpa John bought each of us our own brand new Schwinn bicycle! Cherie got a red one and I got a blue one, and they were beautiful! Mom didn't seem happy about the gifts. It made me nervous that she or Henry would take them away from us. Fortunately, they never did, and we were able to keep our bicycles.

As time went by, Mom was also adding to the division of the relationship between Cherie and me. She would say Cherie looked like her and she wanted to spend time with her. She would treat Cherie like a friend, wanting her to be in the house with her during the day so she could help her clean. They would watch television, eat lunch and snacks together while sending me and my younger siblings outside for me to "amuse" (her words) them. Our younger siblings were toddlers but now old enough to play outside if they had someone supervising them, and I was that supervision. This is where the close relationship and bond with my younger siblings began. Even though they were very young at the time, I had someone in our home who I could love and build a relationship with. I would play with them, care for them, and laugh with them. We became very close. If the weather permitted, we were usually sent outside to play. Outside was safer. As long as I was taking care of our siblings and there wasn't any crying or complaining from them, I was usually left alone.

At lunch time Mom would bring them in the house to eat and sometimes for a nap. For my lunch Mom would usually give me a "doubled over peanut butter sandwich" (one piece of bread with peanut butter spread on it folded in half), handed out the partially opened screen door so I remained outside. Mom could be very cruel to me. If I wanted a drink I could get it out of the hose. I was on my own to figure life out.

CHAPTER 9
THE GREEN RENTAL HOUSE
Nine to Ten Years Old

After a few years, we moved from the old yellow rental house in Valle Vista, California to a green rental house in the same town. It was clean, good sized and had a front yard and a big back yard with both an apricot and a plum tree that produced fruit. It would work well for our family. We were now located a few blocks away from the Valle Vista Store. It was close enough I could walk to the grocery store when Mom needed something. She was a smoker, and often needed me to go to the store and get her a pack of cigarettes. Mom would send me with a handwritten note, requesting that they sell me a package of a particular type of cigarette. Back then they would sell them to a child as long as you had a note from your parent, and the money to pay for them.

The weekend we moved all of our household stuff into the green rental house was rough. During the move, Henry would tell us to pick up one end of a heavy item, like a console television or a heavy dresser, and then he would pick up the other side. These items were too heavy for us, we were just kids. With a very serious and mean voice he would tell us, "Pick it up!" and you knew you better not drop it. Lots of things were too heavy and we struggled to carry the weight of the item or manage the physical size of it. At times, I think it was a miracle we were able to do some of the things that were required of us. But if we dropped it, there would be severe consequences. He did the same thing to Mom, and she struggled also. Sometimes both Cherie and I were on one side and Henry was on the other. This was a job that needed a few strong men, but Cherie, Mom, and I were those few men. Our younger siblings were close to three and four years old when we moved into this house, and too young to help.

Henry settled in to becoming the breadwinner of the family, consistently working full-time. Mom stayed home with us and did odd jobs like ironing for people. Mom would call the local radio station on a certain day of the week, and at a particular time, where she could get free radio time to offer her services for jobs that she could do at home and earn a bit of extra money.

Before long, I met a family in the neighborhood who had a daughter close to my age, and she had a couple of younger siblings that she also had to watch over. It was perfect all the way around. We all became good friends and spent time during the summer, after school, and weekends, running the neighborhood together. This was also perfect for Mom, who put me in charge of "amusing" my younger siblings on those days. It got the three of us kids out of "her hair," especially during the summer when Henry was at work, and she was home.

We would often leave the house in the morning, after breakfast, and head over to meet up with the three neighborhood kids. We played everything that any of us could think of. We would spend our days building forts, petting the donkeys that lived at the end of the street, and carving dirt clods that we gathered in the vacant field next door to our house. We played board games in the garage area and searched for and collected pop bottles that had a refundable return fee, so we could cash them in and buy some penny candy at the Valle Vista Store. We played house or put on shows in our old wooden shed, using one of Grandma McIntire's old quilts as the front curtain for the "stage." We made a water "slip and slide" out of heavy plastic laid out across our grass lawn, with a water hose running on it continuously. We played with our pets. You name it, we did it. It got us out of the house, and we had a lot of fun together. Those are great memories for me.

Mom and Cherie would stay inside and clean the house, do the laundry, and cook dinner. Mom kept a very clean house, and the bills were always paid on time. She ran a tight ship. Henry got paid once a week on Fridays. When he got home from work with his check, she headed out to the bank and the grocery store. She did grocery shopping once a week, getting enough food for the week. If she needed something in the week, she would send me to the Valle Vista store to get it. She was on a tight budget and didn't return to the big grocery store until the following Friday. Mom was an extremely scheduled person. The housecleaning, laundry, and ironing were each scheduled for a certain day of the week. She stuck to that schedule, and nothing changed it.

Once Grandpa John and Grandma Marie retired, they bought a travel trailer so they could tour the United States. When they made it out to California, they took us camping with them for a few days. We had fun with them. They taught us how to play cards and board games. You could see the joy in Grandma Marie's face when we were with them, something that she was really missing in her life. How sad. Grandpa John was a quiet man, you didn't really know what was going on inside of him. They gave us a lot of desired attention that we didn't get at home. Cherie and I both felt their love for us.

There was a nice older man named Walt who Henry worked with at the trailer factory. He was moving to a new place and was only allowed to take one of his two dogs with him. Henry took the other dog and brought it home to us kids. The dog's name was Wimpy. It was a Black female "Cockapoo," a Cocker Spaniel and miniature poodle mix. She was about five years old and had been spayed. She wouldn't be having any puppies, which was perfect. She had curly black hair, short legs, and a wide body. So cute—I adored her! Wimpy was a smart dog and did many tricks. She enjoyed her small rubber blue ball; it was her favorite toy. You could throw that ball as far as you wanted to, and she would fetch it. She would also put out cigarette butts when they were thrown down on the ground and still lit. She would pick it up and shake it, and then drop it, and repeat that until it went out. She was such a joy to us kids. At night she would sleep in an old black chair that was in our screened-in patio, at the back of the house. She wasn't allowed to sleep in our house. I would look out the back door to check on her before I went to bed every night. I could barely see her in the black chair, she blended into it so well with her black fur that I could only see her sweet eyes looking up at me. I loved that dog!

Walt would come over and visit us from time to time. I don't believe he was invited over; I think he just stopped by to see how Wimpy was doing. He would tell us how lucky we were to have a wonderful stepfather like Henry. It was pretty confusing and frustrating to hear those statements. Henry never invited Walt in the house. He would talk with him out in the yard, keeping it short, and before long Walt would leave. Henry and Mom didn't have any friends that came to our house. I don't think Mom had any friends at all. I believe Henry had acquaintances that he only knew from work.

I don't recall it happening right away, but a few years into their marriage Henry began treating Mom badly, physically abusing her. If Mom disagreed with Henry on the way things were going to happen in the household, he would physically hurt her by shoving, hitting, or slapping her. He punished her as though she was a child talking back to him. She didn't do anything to stop it either. Now, looking back, I believe she was afraid of him. He was the boss of the house, and you didn't go against him, even if you were his wife. One time when they came home from the bar, she had a black eye. He had punched her in the face. Another time, I had been told by a family member that at the restaurant he took his foot and pushed her right out of the booth and onto the floor. She stayed at the restaurant with him, and nothing was said or done about it.

At times, Mom would manipulate a situation so she could get me in trouble with Henry. For instance, there was a television show that I liked to watch that aired during the week, in the late afternoon. One day I sat down to watch it and after about five minutes Mom said, "Judy come and take the trash out." I asked if I could wait until the commercial came on, and Mom didn't reply. So I kept watching my show, and when the commercial came on I went to the kitchen to take out the trash, but Mom said, "NO! Leave it, you're not taking it out now." She wouldn't let me. I then went back in to finish watching my show. When Henry came home from work, she told him I had disobeyed her, that I wouldn't take the trash out. Henry got really mad, and then I got punished by him, which is what she wanted to happen to me in the first place.

I can't explain the psychology of why she would do this to me, but I always knew she disliked me, and at times she wanted me to suffer. I was the place where they both could release their anger and rage. I was the child in our family who got blamed for most everything that went wrong.

Around this time Henry began to abuse my younger brother. Once again, it was in the name of "discipline." Henry would whip him with the belt, throw him around, or hit and grab him. He was so young and just starting to experience life. He would make mistakes like all children do, but the punishment was so severe. It was horrible to watch Henry terrorize his son. At this point Cherie was pretty much kept out of Henry's way thanks to Mom. Our youngest sibling was usually mild mannered and for the most part able to stay out of Henry's way by herself, he wasn't focused on her.

Ole Gram and Grandpa came to visit us while we were living in the green house. They made the long trip on the Greyhound bus from Illinois to California. It was the first time they came out to see us. I was so excited that we would be together again. I longed for the loving relationship we shared. I knew they were always out there, just so far away. I was nervous about Henry becoming unglued while they were there, and I was uncertain as to how he would act with them at the house. We never had people come over or stay with us.

It was confusing with Henry; he would react in such extreme ways when he was disciplining, that it seemed and looked like he was totally out of control. But then at the same time, it seemed like he was in full control of what he was doing. That Henry chose to show his anger and rage, reacting so violently while he beat us and threw us around. Henry never let his guard down, he was always quietly monitoring and powerfully controlling the situation at the house. It would be very difficult for Grandpa and Gram to see Henry being abusive to any of us, or Mom. I know in their hearts they were hopeful to have a visit where they saw that their daughter and all of their grandchildren were doing great. But they knew deep down inside, something wasn't right.

We had a wonderful visit. Thankfully, there weren't any incidents with Henry while they were there. He worked most of the time, so he was gone during the days, which worked out well. All too soon they were gone. It was heartfelt, but painful…a moment of what had been, and what could be, but was gone once again. They were always a part of my life through their letters and brief calls. They were there in my thoughts at school, during my lunch time, when I paid for my lunch with money they mailed to us, but I desperately wished they didn't have to leave.

One day a friend and I went for a walk in our neighborhood. I had asked Mom if it was OK that we take a long walk around the block, going over to the next street on the east side, called Fairview. She was OK with it. We were ten years old, just talking and walking together, enjoying the beautiful day. As we walked along the side of Fairview Street, a man came up beside us in his car, slowing down just enough to say something to us. He said, "Hey, come on down to the end of the street, I have some candy for you," and then he picked up speed in his car and drove on down to the end of the street. He parked his car in the citrus grove, where you could barely see him. He was all the way down where the street ended. Fairview Street had houses on large parcels, plus groves of citrus trees in certain areas. Our walk around the block meant we would go in his direction, but shortly we would turn left onto another street to return to my home.

When cars drove down Fairview, he would hide in the grove. Then after they were gone, he would come out into the street and wave his arms motioning for us to come on down to where he was, while yelling out, "COME DOWN HERE!"

The man continued trying to coax us to the end of the street with him. We were continuing to walk along but were starting to feel very uncomfortable with the situation, questioning each other as to what we should do at this point. I quickly turned around to look down the street where we had just walked, and unbelievably, there was a Sheriff's car coming down the road. We flagged him down and he pulled up next to us. We told him what had been going on with the man down the street, who was now hiding again in the citrus grove. The Sheriff instantly sped off in that direction. The man saw the Sheriff's car coming down the road toward him and jumped into his car, speeding out of the citrus grove, and driving across Fairview Street trying to run from the Sheriff. The man then turned left and drove straight across a plowed dirt field, still trying to get away from the Sheriff. He then drove straight up the street I lived on, with the Sheriff following right behind him. The man ended up pulling over to the side of the road, right in front of my house, and the Sheriff arrested him.

My friend and I were running as fast as we could to follow the chase. The man was taken into custody and his vehicle was searched. He had candy, rope, tape, and many other items in his trunk that looked like someone who wanted to abduct a child. He was also from a town that was about twenty minutes away. He had made a special trip to Valle Vista, in an attempt to get two girls into his car. It is very scary to think about.

I was advised by the police department that I would be subpoenaed to go to court and testify against him. I was nervous about it, but I definitely would have done my best. Quite a bit of time passed before we were notified of the court date, maybe a year or so out. I was scheduled to go to court on the following Monday, but he pleaded guilty on the Friday before. I never knew what happened to him, or if he had any prior convictions. But hopefully it helped to get a perpetrator prosecuted and off the street, saving other innocent children from becoming his victims.

I continued to suffer abuse from both Mom and Henry. The sexual abuse stopped shortly after we moved to the green house. I believe it was now more difficult for Henry to find a time to rape me because my younger siblings were getting older, but by continuing to single me out for abuse, my younger siblings were being taught I was just a bad kid, in trouble again, and it was my fault. I deserved this punishment.

Some days were overwhelmingly unbearable for me. I would sit quietly in a hidden spot, in the backyard with my sweet dog Wimpy. I would cradle her on my lap, holding her close, with my face laid across the top of her head. She was my best friend and I loved her. I now understand that she was my support dog. She comforted me during such tough times. I was about nine years old when we got Wimpy, and we had her for almost two years, before a utility truck backed over her by accident. The worker had been installing phone lines near our home and when he went to leave that day, he didn't see her behind the truck. He came to our house and told us what had happened and showed us her lifeless body lying in the back of his truck. He offered to take Wimpy and bury her. My mother agreed to it.

I cried and cried over the loss of Wimpy. There wasn't any comforting or compassion offered by my mother as I grieved. I tried to hide my tears, because I would get humiliated by my mother over crying so much, "over a dog!" My mother told me that we weren't going to get any more animals because I cried too much when they died. She never liked having animals anyway.

CHAPTER 10
MOM AND HENRY BUY THEIR FIRST HOME
Ten Years Old

Mom and Henry had been looking for a house to buy when they came across a "new" gold house with pretty red brick in Hemet, California. No one had lived in it, but it had been used as a model home for prospective buyers. It had four bedrooms, and two bathrooms. Cherie and our younger brother each had their own bedroom now, while I would share a room with my younger sister.

The new house was in a good neighborhood filled with families and was located across from Whittier Elementary School, where I would finish up the last part of my fifth-grade school year. After living in a series of rental houses, we now lived in a house Mom and Henry had bought.

Occasionally, the neighborhood kids would meet up over at the schoolyard to play team sports. We could use the basketball courts, the baseball fields, the blacktop area, or the large green grass fields to run and play. It was a good place to grow up. Back then the schoolyards were left open, which was wonderful for all of us kids to be able to use after school and on the weekends.

My younger brother started kindergarten months after we moved into our new house, and a year later my younger sister started kindergarten. Now all four of us were in public school, so Mom started working outside of the home. She would clean homes for the senior citizens who lived in our community. It was a good job for her, she could make her own hours and could be home when needed. Henry continued his full-time employment at the trailer factory, which was now only a five-minute drive from the new house.

Henry continued to punch, slap, grab, shove, hit me with the belt, or throw me down the hall if I did or said something that made him mad. One thing I didn't like about the new house was the kitchen sink faced the wall. I couldn't see who was coming up behind me while I was washing dishes. Henry would quietly walk up behind me, put his hands around my neck, and begin squeezing. He would apply pressure on the front of my neck with his fingers, which would make me pass out. Prior to passing out I would feel dizzy, get a weird taste in my mouth, and a weakened sensation in my body, and down I would go. Henry would catch me before I fell to the ground. He would laugh about it. He was thrilled that he could make me pass out. I was shaken by the level of power Henry had over me and my physical body. Again, he could do anything he wanted to me. It was difficult to exist under the stress of these living conditions.

It was similar to being a prisoner, Henry's prisoner. The trauma from this continues to affect me in my adult life.

Sometimes our younger brother would ask to sleep with me and our younger sister. He was young, around five years old, and just wanted to be in the same room with us. Henry would allow him to sleep in our room, but also told us that we weren't allowed _any_ talking. We were to go directly to sleep. The kids were young, and our brother would whisper and giggle. When Henry would hear him, he would yell, "Go to sleep!" one time, and one time only, with an angry voice. I would be so afraid for our brother and wish that he would just go to sleep. Of course, our brother would whisper something again, and that was it for Henry. He would jump up from the couch, rapidly pull his leather belt out of his pants, and angrily stomp down the hall toward our room. Henry would grab our brother and yank him up and out of the bed, whipping him severely with the belt. He would carry him down the hall to his bedroom and throw him on his bed. Then Henry would yell, "Now go to sleep!" Our brother would be crying inconsolably. It was horrible. My younger sister and I would be traumatized by the whole event, frozen in fear and lying very still in our bed. Henry would return to his seat in the living room and continue to watch television like he did every night. This same circumstance happened a few times, and sadly with the same outcome.

Once we moved to this house, Henry became very regimented. Monday through Friday he would get up in the morning at the very same time and follow the same routine every day. He would shower, get dressed, go to work, come home, take a shower, put on clean clothes — a white T-shirt, jeans, and socks — then sit at the dinner table, and dinner better be ready at that time too, or again there would be hell to pay.

We would all eat dinner together each night, but we didn't really talk much because everyone was always nervous. If any of us accidentally knocked over our glass of water or spilled something else during dinner, we would be punished. Nothing was just an accident; you were obviously fooling around. It was your fault; it ruined the meal and there would be a consequence.

If one of us kids did something "wrong" earlier that day, then Mom would usually bring it up at the dinner table. It was so nerve-racking to worry all day that Mom might say something, it would make us physically ill.

After Henry finished eating, he would get up from the table, go sit on the couch with his feet on the coffee table, watch television until about 9:50 p.m. (not talking or moving around, just staring at the TV), and then get up and go to bed and do the same thing the next day. If he were interrupted in any way during this time, it would anger him. If you walked past the television (which was next to the front door) to go outside too many times, then you were told you had to stay in the house and you couldn't go outside anymore that evening.

On the weekends, during Henry's days off from work, his schedule was a bit different. Instead of going off to work, he would get up and shower as usual, and then go to the table to eat breakfast. He would pour a bowl of dry cereal, and then sometimes tell Cherie or me to pour milk on his cereal. This meant one of us getting up from the table and grabbing the milk carton, then going over and standing next to Henry to pour it. If the milk bounced off a Corn Flake and onto his clean shirt, he would explode! He would begin cussing and reacting physically, knocking everything off the kitchen table in one fast swipe, or sometimes he would throw the table up and everything would fly off, going everywhere. Angrily, he would walk away from the mess he had just created as though it was justified because of the milk making a stain on his shirt. We would have to clean it up. It always made everyone else in the house completely frazzled. He changed his shirt and left the house immediately, alone, sometimes slamming the door and screeching out of the driveway. Maybe that was his plan all along, to get out of the house by himself without Mom?! She definitely wouldn't question him about anything at that point.

If the milk didn't get spilled on Henry's shirt and breakfast was over, he might go to the local swap meet (flea market). Or he might just sit and watch television all day. He would sit there on the couch, staring at the television, with his feet on the coffee table, and never saying anything all day, just like he did on the weekdays. If Henry were home at lunch time on Saturday or Sunday, and I was in the house, I would have to make his lunch. Usually, he wanted me to make him a tuna salad sandwich. If he found a hair in any of the food that was prepared for him, look out! No telling what might happen to the person who made the food. Or the bread wasn't right, or the tuna salad didn't have enough pickles. He would explode about things like that. I would be as careful as I could, but sometimes things like that just happen. He was a ticking time bomb ready to blow at any moment.

Henry and Mom started going out in the evenings on the weekend for dinner, drinks, and dancing. During this period there was a couple that Mom and Henry hung out with. They were their partying friends, and they would all meet at the bar and restaurant. I believe these people were originally Henry's friends, but I don't know where or how their relationship got started. Our family was invited over to their house many times, and we did go over and we kids became friends with their children. It was fun to play at their house because there were things to do, and children our age to play with. They had a Doughboy pool, mini-bikes, and a horse we could ride. This is where I was swimming the day that Henry put his hands down my pants and fondled me in the pool, over at his friend's house. What a brazen act. There were other kids all around, including my siblings, and he still sexually assaulted me. He was an arrogant, sick perpetrator who now felt confident enough to abuse me in public.

Their family was never invited to our house. Mom didn't like having anyone over, especially children. It didn't seem like she really liked children at all, even though she had four of them. As far as she was concerned, they would just make a mess in her house, and she liked her house kept spotless. I don't think she ever experienced the joy in children, her own or others. She didn't let our cousins come in our house either, even when they lived in our neighborhood. If they were thirsty, they had to get a drink of water out of the hose outside.

I spent a lot of time with my younger siblings, we were close and played together almost every day. I could be creative and I found things for us to do that would be fun. We would do crafts like making things from pieces of wood we found at the construction sites around our home. We rode our bikes everywhere, sometimes up town to different stores, or the library. We sold pecans that we collected from our pecan trees out front. We would make and then fly our kites over in the schoolyard. We did our best to keep busy and out of Mom and Henry's way. Cherie was usually busy doing her own thing, away from us. She was going one way in life, and the three of us were going in another direction. None of us had much of a relationship with her. If she were at home, she would usually be in her bedroom with the door closed, not interacting with us.

I had become a kid who could be funny and make others laugh, especially my siblings. Humor and laughter helped me cope with the difficult life I was living. At school I was quiet until I got to know people, and then my funny side would come out. At home I still walked on eggshells when I was around Mom and Henry, trying to evaluate their mood so I knew how to act.

When school was out for the summer, and all the other kids were elated that they would be home for three months, I anguished over what might happen to me during that time. I have memories of sitting outside, looking around the neighborhood, watching the other kids running happily through their yards, laughing and playing, seeming like they didn't have a worry in the world. I longed to feel that way…the joy of childhood and to be valued by my parents. I often thought I would have given *anything* to just have a "normal life."

CHAPTER 11
JUNIOR HIGH SCHOOL
Eleven to Thirteen Years Old

I was now in my first year of junior high school. Through the years I had learned that I was on my own as far as school, including my projects and homework. I was still expected to get good grades, but there wasn't any help from home. If I asked my mother for help, I was bothering her, and she wasn't really interested in helping anyway. I didn't ask Henry, because the whole household revolved around his needs and wants, and they did not include helping any of us kids with anything. Neither parent attended open houses in our classrooms nor award assemblies. If the teacher scheduled one, Mom would go to parent/teacher conferences, otherwise once Mom and Henry got home from work, they didn't leave the house.

I was deeply under Henry's control at this point in my life. The pain, torture, and abuse he inflicted on me kept me there. It was 1970, and there wasn't anything on television about child abuse that would have educated me as to what abuse is or that it is against the law. If that information was out there, I never saw it. This was just how my life was. I didn't have a voice or a say in any situation. My voice had been suppressed a long time ago. I learned that if I tried to speak up about anything, I would be physically hurt and then punished. It had gotten to a point where I couldn't speak up for myself without having a strong physical reaction of anxiety and panic. When I didn't defend myself as I was being falsely accused of something, I would feel a lump in my throat, my chest would get tight, and tears would roll down my face. I would be ready to burst. I tried to be silent and go with the flow, but most of the time it was difficult to just stand there when you knew something wasn't the truth.

My physical education class in junior high school required me to change into athletic clothing daily, along with all the other girls in the locker room. I didn't always want to undress, because at times I would have bruises or marks on my body from being "punished," sometimes from being whipped with the belt by Henry, but I had to. If I had visible marks on my body, I would carefully hide them with my clothing, moving it around to cover me as I changed. Usually, they were on my butt and thighs, but sometimes on my back. They could be bruises in the shape of belt marks, that occasionally broke through the skin. I was too embarrassed for the other students to see the marks on my body because I felt that they were going to judge me, confirming that I had done something wrong and I deserved the marks. It would be one more validation that I was a bad kid who didn't follow the rules. I didn't need anything else to add to my low self-worth. It is sad to think back on the fact that I hid the marks. It illustrates just how scared and confused I was at this age. I also had no reason to trust grown-ups.

Mom and Henry's relationship was worse than it had ever been. Sometimes on the weekend, he would go out without her, and not come home all day. She wouldn't have any idea where he had gone. She would call around to different places, usually bars, to see if he was there, and if he was, she would ask that they put him on the phone. Once on the phone, she would ask him to come home. This never went over well with him. She was embarrassing him, and no one told Henry what to do. He wouldn't come home right away, but when he did get home, they would fight about it. I was embarrassed for her, and the fact that she thought she should call around looking for him. Henry knew where we lived; he knew his way home.

Mom spent a lot of time and energy trying to get Henry's attention, but he wasn't interested in her, and never wanted her affection. He would be dishonest to her, and he didn't communicate with her, or show her any respect. He actually didn't give her the time of day. I never thought he was in love with her, and I never saw anything that resembled love between them. He did give a lot of the wrong types of attention to me though, and it wasn't parental attention.

Henry began taking me with him on Saturday mornings to the swap meet or over to visit his friend. He would only take me, and it made me nervous as to what this was all about. What was he up to? One day when we were alone at home he talked to me about keeping my ears clean, saying, "Just in case you get a boyfriend, you would want them to be clean." He made me feel so uneasy. I knew he had complete control over me. I didn't want him near me, to look at me, or even think thoughts like that about me. I just wanted him to leave me alone, but he didn't.

At home Henry would make me come and sit right next to him on the couch, and then he would put his arm around me, which I hated; it gave me anxiety and caused even more grief for me with Mom. This would make Mom so angry; she would tell me to get up, and he would tell me to stay put. I didn't want to sit next to him. I hated him, but I didn't have any choice. I was stuck in the middle of their dysfunctional relationship, and I feared him more than her, so I just did what he said and dealt with her consequences later. Our counselor said this was a typical incest dynamic, "Mother's disdain for the other woman" — her daughter.

Cherie got a job at a fast-food restaurant when she was fourteen years old. She could earn some money and it got her out of the house. This was the beginning of her becoming more independent. Before long she became a "Candy Striper" at the local hospital, a volunteer who helps the nursing staff. Mom would give her rides to her job or the hospital, or sometimes she would get a ride from a friend.

Henry was a ticking time bomb that could go off at any moment. I learned to carefully pay attention to Henry and Mom's moods. My counselor said he has noticed that kids who have grown up in abusive situations develop this almost radar-like quality, an ability to read the moods of other people, particularly people who might have power or authority over them in some way. They get particularly good at doing that and acting accordingly, adjusting to the mood as they see it.

Henry enjoyed upsetting Mom. Sometimes he would have me hide in the coat closet by the front door. When Mom came home and opened the closet door to put her coat away, I would jump out and scare her. It would frighten her and then she would be very mad at me. Henry thought it was funny, and he forced me to do it. If I didn't, I would face consequences from him. Even in this type of situation I did what he told me to do. I knew better than to go against him or make him mad. You put yourself in danger if he was mad at you. I was constantly a pawn in their dysfunctional relationship.

A few times after Mom had been physically abused by Henry, she would tell me we were going to move out, and that she was done. But the next day, when I would quietly ask her when we were going to move out, she would reply to me in a condescending voice, that she wasn't going to leave all this stuff (the furniture and household contents, etc.), that I was stupid for thinking that! Mom was really into material things and money; she was focused on those things more than any of her children. Each time, I would become extremely hopeful we might leave, but she never left Henry.

Mom's life was miserable, but she continued to choose that misery. She told us she was depressed so her doctor prescribed medication to help her. She called this medication her nerve pills. She could have contacted family for help, and we would have all been rescued from a terrible situation, but she chose not to. I think she never wanted to admit she made a mistake, following a second man to another state. She would rather stay in a bad situation, leaving all of us in it too.

There were times where she would tell the four of us kids that if it weren't for us, she would kill herself. I honestly felt nothing when she said this. I thought "here she goes again, putting her children in a bad situation." It was always all about her. How were any of us supposed to process that, let alone the younger ones who were probably seven and eight years old at the time. I was unable to find any compassion for her and so I just wouldn't say anything when she brought up suicide. After so many years of neglect, I didn't have any good feelings toward her. She hadn't ever shown she loved or cared about me. Not when my leg was broken, not when Henry beat me severely, not when he was holding me over the toilet to vomit, after forcing me to drink hard alcohol at six years old, not when my dog Wimpy was killed, NEVER.

Mom wasn't a kind and loving person. She was selfish and her focus was always on what would benefit her. I remember the cruel comments that came out of her mouth, as she found pleasure in the fact that someone was going through a difficult time. I heard her speak that way many times, and one of those times it was about a close family member. I always felt sickened by her awful behavior.

As I became a teenager, my mind was changing, my body was changing, and my own interests were getting stronger. I just wanted to be normal and to be able to do the things my peers were doing.

There was a period of time, I believe a week, where I had to stay after school to complete a project, so I couldn't ride the regular bus home. We lived at least five miles from the school, so Mom had to pick me up on each of these days. Mom told me that during this week, she wasn't going to pick me up from school until Henry called her from work, when he needed a ride home, which was usually about 5 to 5:30 p.m. Henry's employer was west from our house, about a five-minute drive, and my school was east from our house about a fifteen-minute drive. The after-school session was over at about 3:30 p.m. So, each day I had to wait until Mom got the call from Henry, and then she would come to pick me up. I also couldn't just sit on the grass in front of the school waiting for her. I was told that I needed to wait on the busy street corner where the school was located, just in case she came early, so I could just jump in the car when she stopped at the four-corner stop sign. That way she could pick up Henry as soon as possible.

This meant that each day I leaned on a fire hydrant that was located on a busy four-corner stop, for one to two hours until she came to get me. This was clearly a form of child neglect. There I was, a thirteen-year-old girl standing on a busy street corner so that Mom wouldn't waste any gas, or any time, by pulling in the school parking lot. The awful part about it is that we weren't poor either. Mom was just so cheap she wouldn't use the extra gasoline or time to pick me up when I was done. I wasn't important enough.

In eighth grade I met a new friend at school who, like me, loved to laugh and be silly. She could be so funny, and we quickly became best friends. We were both thirteen years old and in the same drama class. We became known for creating and performing our drama skits as a team. Her friendship brought a lot of laughter and joy to my life during the school day. I always looked forward to going to school to see her and spend time together.

I also took a sewing class and loved it. I learned the basics of sewing and completed a few required projects. We had a foot pedal sewing machine at home but no one in our family used it or knew how to sew. I think it was Grandma McIntire's. Before long, I learned how to sew on it and began making different things out of material. Sometimes I would use scraps of material I was given, or I would cut up old clothing and make something new out of it. If I had money, I would buy yardage and patterns. I loved to sew and spent any time I could mending or making different things for the family and myself. I also took a class in knitting and crocheting. These skills helped to keep my mind busy and productive in a positive way.

Quite often Henry would put Cherie down. He would just say mean things about her. It was obvious he didn't like her, or he was mad at her, probably because she had told Mom about him sexually molesting her. The unkind things he would say to her would hurt my heart. One time I helped her sew a dress and when she went to show him the finished product, he laughed and made fun of it. He said it looked like a potato sack. He was just cruel and hateful. I believe this was his calculating way to get back at her. The weird thing with me is he abused me the most, on all levels, but he wouldn't put me down. He would tell me I was the smart one and that I was the only one who would amount to anything.

Throughout the years my siblings and I spent time attending church. On Sunday morning Mom would drop all of us off at Sunday School and pick us up after it was over. Sometimes we would also attend the church service. She told us that she had already put her time in at church and didn't need to go herself. In many ways church was really the saving grace because it was a safe place where I could spend time with other people socializing, learning, and having fun away from home. If I wanted to attend the events that happened in the evening at church, I would have to ride my bicycle both to and from the event. The ride home was always in the dark. It was about a twenty-minute ride, one way.

I was always trying to figure out how to succeed in this dysfunctional household. When the school library had their annual book sale there was an older set of encyclopedias for a very cheap price. I decided to purchase them because they would be a good resource to have at home, plus they would help with our schoolwork. I paid for them, and then the librarian agreed to let me carry a handful of the books home on the school bus each day, until I got all of them home. It would have been too big of a deal for Mom to come and help me get them home, so I didn't bother asking.

The librarian was good with that plan and set the books aside for me. There were about twenty-two large heavy books. It was a journey carrying them out of the library and onto the school bus and then home from where I got dropped off at my bus stop. But I did it in about three days. I set them up in consecutive order against one wall in my bedroom. I was really happy to have them, and I used them often.

As I became a teenager, I was quite involved in the church youth group which included many social events and outings like going to Disneyland or ice skating or summer church retreats. I usually had to come up with the money for these events, but since it was through the church, I could go. Church helped keep my sanity, giving me guidance and a social life. As a teenager, between Sunday school, church, youth group, Bible study and special outings, I could get out of the house more often. Cherie also liked to attend some of the youth group activities or events. I invited my best friend to come to youth group with me and before long she regularly attended the church meetings and events too. When we had fundraisers at church, like a spaghetti dinner for everyone, my best friend and I would provide the entertainment. We would act out funny skits for the audience. We both enjoyed it.

Our second and last trip back to Illinois to visit our family occurred in August of 1972. Once again we drove our car there and back. Cherie was now sixteen years old; I was thirteen years old; our younger brother was seven years old, and our younger sister was six years old. During the visit Uncle Butch and Aunt Merikay took all of us kids to Santa's Village for the day. It was a fun trip, and I still have the pictures to bring back the memories. It was great to see our family, but again it was a quick visit, and I couldn't say a word about our life in California. The fear of Henry always stopped me in my tracks. Once again, feeling hopeless, I cried all the way back to California.

When I was between thirteen and sixteen years old, Henry started what I believe was a new approach. I would come home by myself from my church youth group in the evening, at about

9:30 p.m. He would be the only one still awake in the house and once again if the opportunity arose where he could approach me when no one was around, he would. He would hug me and tell me how much he loved me. I hated him, but also feared him and had learned that I always needed to deal with any situation that involved him very carefully. He was mentally ill, and he had complete control over my life. In some sick way I think he was trying to seduce me, thinking that this approach to having sexual contact with me could be consensual. Fortunately, I was always able to get away from him.

Gram & Grandpa Byers in Illinois, leaving for California 1972

CHAPTER 12
GRAM AND GRANDPA MOVE TO HEMET, CALIFORNIA!
Fourteen Years Old

I couldn't believe it! Gram and Grandpa were moving to Hemet, California, where we lived! They would be selling the farm in Illinois. Wow, I was so excited that they would live by us. I would finally have them back in my life, they would save me, they were always my only hope. I loved them so much and couldn't believe it. It was a dream come true. Later in life I would find out they knew something wasn't right in California, and instead of following their original plan to retire in Florida, they gave all of that up to move to California where they could see what was really going on.

During the nine years that my grandparents continued to live in Illinois, they were always in my heart and a big part of my life. I missed them terribly. We only visited them twice during this time, and I believe they were only able to come out to California once to visit us. Otherwise, we spoke on the phone, had communication by mail every week, and received a special package or mailing for every holiday and birthday. In the early years, Gram would ask us to draw the outline of our feet on a piece of paper and mail it to her so they could buy us Easter shoes and clothing to wear to church on Easter Sunday. They never forgot an important moment. Their love and support was amazing. Knowing that they were out there gave me hope for a day when things might be different. I was blessed with already having experienced their unconditional love and I desperately needed it back in my life.

Mom occasionally called Gram and Grandpa and each of us would visit with them for a couple of minutes. I never wanted to talk on the phone to them because it made me so emotional. Hearing their voices caused me to miss them even more. When it was my time to talk, Mom held the phone up to my ear and stood right next to me saying, "Hurry, hurry, hurry up! These phone calls are expensive!" My mind would be racing about what to say, while trying to stay focused, and answer their questions without crying. I would always have a big lump in my throat, trying to hold back the tears. Sadly, there wasn't ever enough time on the phone for a heartfelt visit with our grandparents. As usual, money was the main focus as each telephone minute ticked by. When the visit was over and we hung up the phone, I knew it was as painful for my grandparents as it was for me.

The communication by mail was weekly on Gram's part, she was truly remarkable. Every week she would mail us a big yellow envelope that included a handwritten letter, candy and gum for us kids, and lunch money for the week for Cherie and me, wrapped up individually in a white piece of ruled paper with our names written on it. This package would come every Friday or Saturday for years. Once in a while, it would not come until Monday, because she got it out too late that week. I would watch for the mail carrier on those days to see if it came. If that happened and it did not come by Saturday, I would ask the mail carrier, "Are you sure it isn't in your mail truck?! I know she sent it!" As a kid I did not understand how it all worked, and I knew my Ole Gram wouldn't forget us, so it had to be the mail carriers fault. It must have been in his truck underneath something and he just missed it! It was such a reminder and a connection to my old life that I was desperately clinging on to. Her packages proved someone thought of and cared for us. Knowing they were still out there loving us unconditionally because we were important gave us hope.

There was a short time period where Gram included extra money in the weekly manila envelope to pay for my twirling baton lessons. Gram and I had discussed this on the phone and in letters. I enjoyed twirling the baton, so she had encouraged me to take lessons so that maybe someday I could perform in the front of the parade. They had also given me a baton, which I still have today. I found someone who gave lessons, but it would have required some effort and driving on her part, so Mom never signed me up. Some time went by where Gram thought I was taking the baton lessons, and she was still sending the money to pay for them. Eventually Mom had to tell her I wasn't taking them. I don't know what her excuse was, and then we spent Gram's baton lesson money on something else.

Now that Grandpa and Gram were living in Hemet, they told us they had a few gifts they had planned on getting for Cherie and me. They believed girls our age should have new ten-speed bicycles so we could get around more easily, so they bought them for us. They also thought we should have our own sleeping bags, for the church camping trips or sleepovers at a friend's house, so they bought those for us too. Since I had learned to sew, they felt I deserved a new electric sewing machine and bought me one. WOW! I was still sewing on the old foot pedal sewing machine. We were thrilled to get all of these nice and helpful gifts. It was wonderful! We never got much from Henry and Mom, just the basic needs.

Of course, now that they lived nearby, my grandparents wanted to visit us often, but Mom and Henry never asked people over, so I wondered how this was going to work out with my grandparents.

Henry lived his life how he wanted to, especially in HIS home. The behavior he exhibited as a father, husband, and man would obviously conflict with my grandparents' way of treating people. He wasn't going to be sent to the store, he wouldn't be helping in the kitchen, and he absolutely wouldn't ever wash a dish or take the trash out. All of these tasks were beneath him. Also, he was going to treat us kids like he always did, including Mom. No one was going to tell him differently. One time we were out of laundry detergent and Gram mentioned that we could send Henry to the store and get it. It was just the two of us talking, so no one else heard it, but it took my breath away to think how he might react if she said that to him.

At first the visits were here and there on the weekends. But before long, my grandfather was going with Mom and Henry to the cocktail lounge/restaurant they frequented Friday or Saturday night. A few months went by, and Grandpa had gone to the bar many times with them. There was dancing and drinking, and it was usually a late-night event. Either Cherie or I babysat our siblings during these outings. Honestly, we looked forward to the weekend nights when they would go out and leave us at home.

At about 2 a.m. on one of the nights that they went out, I was awakened by the screeching of tires as their car came into the garage. I heard Mom and Henry come into the house, and Henry was angry. It sounded like Mom was trying to plead and reason with him. My heart was racing not knowing what was going on. Before long Mom was continually crying out that she had pain and that her heart was hurting bad, she felt like she was having a heart attack. These sounds of anguish coming out of Mom's mouth went on for at least a couple of hours. I heard a lot of discussion and arguing and then silence. The next day we were told that Grandpa and Gram were not allowed to come over to our home any longer. I was shocked, scared, and saddened. I knew something happened at the bar.

It would be a while before I was told what had happened. Eventually Mom and Henry gave in and would let us go over and visit Gram and Grandpa once in a while, but it was by Mom and Henry's "bizarre" rules (Henry's, I'm sure) that we could make these visits. We had to walk down to the end of our block where Gram could pick us up. She was not allowed to park in front of our house. I guess Henry controlled the street in front of our house too. Gram did not like it at all but went along with it so she and Grandpa could see us.

Once I could visit, I found out Grandpa had only gone to the bar with them so he could find out who Henry really was, by spending time with him. Henry would flirt with other women, among other behaviors, so Grandpa called him out that night telling Henry, "You can't pull the wool over my eyes...I know who you are." Henry did not like people standing up to him, so that made him very mad, and he never spoke to Grandpa again. I don't believe Mom ever spoke to her father again after that night. This was less than two years after they had moved out to California to live by us. Honestly, I was surprised it lasted that long. Henry was always going to be in control.

Grandpa Byers and Judy fourteen-fifteen years old, 1972-73?

CHAPTER 13
GROWING UP
Fifteen Years Old

L ife at home continued, Henry was the boss, and Mom followed his lead. We could only visit Gram and Grandpa once in a while, which was awful for them. They were older, had health problems, and had moved their entire life out to California to be with us. They had left their family and longtime friends behind in Illinois. It was difficult for me also, because out of the four grandchildren, I had the closest relationship with them. My younger siblings didn't really know Gram and Grandpa, having only spent a few days here and there together. Cherie was connected to them, but not as much as I was.

Before long, I learned how to sew on the new machine and began making all kinds of clothing and material items. It helped to take my mind off what was going on at home and gave me a sense of achievement. One summer I sewed my younger siblings' school clothes for the following year. Mom purchased the yardage, patterns, and sewing notions and I sewed the clothing. This was more economical for Mom, and I enjoyed making them, so it all worked out. Everything I made wasn't perfect for sure, but I was learning as I went along. I also sewed Cherie's long dresses for her school dances, including the prom. Plus, I sewed a short-sleeved men's shirt for her boyfriend to wear to her school dance, which was made of the same print as her long dress. It was popular back then to use the same print for the dress and man's shirt. I also sewed for myself, and I made a few things for Mom.

My younger siblings and I continued to spend a lot of time together at home, and in the neighborhood. Each of us also had a best friend. My younger sister's best friend lived right next door, so it was easy for them to play together. My younger brother had a best friend who lived in the neighborhood, and he could go over to his house, or the friend could come over once in a while. They also saw their best friends at school. I had the same best friend since eighth grade. She lived across town. I would see her at school, and once in a while I could go to her house and visit. While we could occasionally have a friend visit, there were weird, strict rules. If they came over, they were only allowed to stay for a few hours, and the time that they could come and go was pretty much set in stone. We always had to play outside. Of course, everyone had to drink out of the hose if they were thirsty. It was always a "big deal" for Mom to allow anyone to come over, and the rules were embarrassing.

It was rare for me to have a friend spend the night. The rules I had to follow and the fear of something going wrong wasn't worth it. For instance, when I was a teenager and my best friend came over to spend the night, she would not be "allowed" to come over until about 7:00 p.m. and we had to go to bed at 9-9:30 p.m. She then had to leave between 7:30 and 8 a.m. the next morning. Then Mom would say, "You had your fun, now you need to do chores or yardwork." It was as though you had to pay to have fun?! It worked the same way when I wanted to stay the night at a friend's house. I could go over (ride my bicycle to her house miles away) after I washed the dinner dishes, and then I needed to be home the next morning at 7:30 a.m. or 8:00 a.m., if I was lucky… (I was riding back home on my bicycle). If I argued about it, then I would not be able to go at all. If it was worth it I just had to shut my mouth and go with it. I think my best friend stayed the night only once or twice, and I was a nervous wreck the whole time. If I were allowed to go, I would spend the night at her house. At least it was fun and normal when I got there. I just had to make sure I was home on time the next morning. If I were late at all, I would be punished.

Cherie was very busy with school, her job, and her boyfriend. She came and left the house all the time. Her boyfriend would pick her up and take her to school and work and then bring her back home, after work. That was perfect for Mom, she didn't have to give her rides to and from work. Cherie had become very independent; she had a lot of freedom and could pretty much do what she wanted to at this point. Mom kept Cherie out of the main functions of the house such as cooking, cleaning, yard work and babysitting. This helped to take Cherie out of Henry's radar.

One morning right after Cherie came home from an all-night school event, Henry told her she needed to mow the lawn. This was odd since he'd mostly left Cherie alone at this point, but maybe he felt the need to remind us he was always in control. To my surprise, Mom spoke up and said, "No! Judy can go out and mow the lawn, Cherie hasn't slept all night. She needs to go to bed." Mom was willing to stand up for Cherie at times, whereas she wouldn't do that for me. Henry physically hit Mom that morning for "arguing" with him, and then told Cherie that she was going to do what he said. Cherie went out and mowed the lawn. I felt bad for her. I don't remember a situation like that ever happening again between Henry and Cherie.

I was kept home most of the time on the weekends, because Henry and Mom "might" decide to go out drinking and dancing, and if they did, they needed me to babysit my younger siblings. It felt very unfair to me. I never felt like my life was important. It was difficult as a teenager.

Mom would constantly discuss how many years each of us had until we were eighteen and would be leaving the house. She was counting the years until she wasn't raising any more children, until she was done. Henry would say, "And don't bring any grandkids back here either."

We had a stray dog come by the house one day and I begged to keep him. He was the first dog we were able to have since Wimpy. We named him Fritz; he was a mixed breed who looked like a brown Dachshund but with a larger body and longer legs. He loved to jump up on top of his doghouse and hang out there. I loved Fritz; he was happy and lots of fun. One day I came home from school to find out that my mom had called the dog catcher to pick him up and take him away. In the joy of a young dog, he had jumped up and torn some of her clothing as it was dancing in the wind on the clothesline. I was heartbroken.

CHAPTER 14
SUICIDE ATTEMPT-END OF THE SUMMER
Fifteen Years Old

In the summer of 1974, when I was fifteen years old, I attempted suicide. I had come to a point in my life where I could not go on living like I had been for the past ten years. I just could not do it. I could not live with Mom or Henry having power or control over me any longer. I could not emotionally or physically handle any more pain or suffering. I could not live with the anxiety of not knowing what was going to happen to me next, what pain I would suffer, what cruel and merciless child abuse I would be expected to endure.

What was the point of life, if it was not ever going to get any better? Maybe it would improve when I was an adult and out of there. But at fifteen years old that seemed like it wasn't ever going to happen. I didn't think I could make it that long; I couldn't make it another day. I didn't want to die; I just couldn't live like this anymore. I was completely overwhelmed and wanted out of this situation any way I could get out. At the time, suicide seemed like the only way out.

I began searching the house for pills. I probably had only taken an aspirin or two in my lifetime, so I wasn't familiar with pills or their reactions. I knew Mom took pills to help her sleep and I found them under the sink in her bathroom. I also found a bottle of aspirin. There weren't very many sleeping pills left in the bottle, but I took them all. I also took a lot of aspirin — as many as I could get down. Before long I was asleep on my bed, and I slept most of the day. My two younger siblings who were eight and nine years old at the time, were the only ones home that day. Mom and Henry were at work and Cherie was out. I would wake up off and on. When I did, my head felt hollow and numb and I was very sleepy. I would then doze off again and before long I would wake back up.

I didn't want to wake up in this world anymore I wanted to wake up with things different, with a new life, a safe life...but of course, I didn't. Nothing had changed except that it was later in the day and Mom and Henry would be home soon. I heard Cherie's voice in the distance and knew she was now home. My head was still numb, and my body felt weird and sleepy. I now heard Mom's voice; she was home also.

I began to feel afraid of what I had done. I thought I should at least tell Cherie. She was getting ready to go to work at the hospital, where she was employed in the business department. Cherie looked shocked when I told her, and she immediately went and told Mom what I had done, and that I needed to go to the hospital. Cherie finished getting ready and went on to work. I was now even more scared that she told Mom. I lay quietly in my room, feeling off.

Mom was sitting in her lounge chair in the living room. She didn't budge when Cherie told her about me. Instead of quickly walking down the hall and coming into my room with concern for my well-being, she began yelling loudly for me to come out there in the living room, saying in her demanding and uncompassionate voice that she wanted to talk to me.

I was lying down in my bedroom, which was the last room down the hall, and I could hear her loud and clear. I got up, feeling fuzzy headed, and went out there. She asked me what I had done, and I told her. She got mad at me and began lecturing me on how she needs those medications to sleep and how dare I take those because now she doesn't have them to use! She grounded me for taking the pills. She didn't ask me how I felt or mention going to the hospital. She was just thinking about herself and the loss of the medications. Henry was due home shortly and I knew she would tell him I took all the pills, and I worried about that, A LOT.

When Henry got home, she told him what I had done. His reaction was much different than I thought it would be. He was quiet and didn't say much. I think he was afraid of the attention that this could have brought to the abuse. He didn't mention going to the hospital or ask how I was doing. The evening just went on as usual and by the next day I felt pretty much back to normal, the effect of the medication was gone. But the deep feeling that I couldn't live under their control and their abuse was stronger than ever. I had to do something. I had to get out of there. I was ready to tell my secret.

CHAPTER 15
THE TRUTH WILL SET YOU FREE
Sixteen Years Old

U p to this point, I hadn't told anyone what I had been going through for the past eleven years. No one, not my best friend, no family members or teachers or even anyone at the church. I had also just met a guy at school named Brian, and we were developing a relationship, but I didn't tell him either. Cherie and I still hadn't ever discussed that each of us had been sexually abused by Henry. We really never talked about anything. I wanted to tell other people, but I was so afraid of Henry and what he might do to me, that I didn't. My Gram used to say that there are worse things than death, and it truly applies here. I was afraid of being tortured and injured by Henry. He was cruel and mean and had no regard for my life. From the beginning he had made it clear to me that I better not tell ANYONE ANYTHING! The perpetrator stole my sense of trust, and I now needed trust to escape the perpetrator.

I just couldn't go on like this any longer. I needed to do something that would change my life, change my living situation. But I also had to get up enough courage to tell someone. I decided to tell my best friend. We had now been best friends for three years and I trusted her. Afterward we both went to the school psychologist/counselor, and I then told him. I will never forget him or that moment. I briefly told the counselor what Henry had done to me through the years while I lived with him and was under his care. I felt extremely nervous, scared, and hopeful as I spoke my truth. The counselor then sent my friend back to class and we continued to talk. He asked me if I had a healthy place where I could go and live. He said that the law allowed for this at my age. I said, "YES! My grandparents' home." He said OK and that I would have to tell them about the abuse, and that I would need to tell them everything.

I hated the thought of having to share the abusive events of my childhood with them. I knew how much it would hurt them. The counselor said that we would need to call my grandparents and ask them to come to the school for a meeting with him and me, in his office.

That was one of the hardest discussions I have ever had. We agreed they'd come to the school a few days later to meet with me and the counselor. I will never forget the look on their faces that day as they walked into the counselor's office. It was an incredibly sad day. How horrible for them to find out that their two young granddaughters had been living in such an abusive situation for all these years in California, after they left their loving farm in Illinois. Also, the realization that their daughter, our mother, allowed it to happen. They were both horrified, angry, overwhelmed, and just plain sad as they listened to me speak about the abuse.

My grandparents were elderly, in their seventies, and had medical problems. Grandpa had rheumatoid arthritis all over his body, it wasn't easy for him to physically walk into the school, or to be able to cope with what he was hearing. Gram also had health problems and now they were also going to be raising their sixteen-year-old granddaughter and fighting their own daughter for the right to do it. They both agreed that I was welcome to live with them, there wasn't even a question.

The counselor laid out the plan. I would spend the upcoming weekend at my home and then on Monday I would return to school. After school on Monday, I would go home and tell my mother that I was moving out because of the abusive situation and that I would be going to live with my maternal grandparents. My grandmother would pick me up at 4 p.m. that day. I would be packed and ready. Henry wouldn't be off work until 5p.m., so I should be out of there before he got home, which I was extremely nervous about. I absolutely had to be out of there before he got home.

However, there was one stipulation made by the counselor. I was to tell my mother about all the abuse that had happened to me while I was left in Henry's care. I was to do this before I left home for good on Monday afternoon. I agreed and knew that timewise, I would have to tell Mom on Friday afternoon, right after I got home from school, but before Henry got home from work. It would be too risky to tell her while Henry was home. Friday afternoon was my only time because Henry had weekends off. After school on Monday, I would quickly pack my things, and then tell Mom that I was leaving to go and live with Gram and Grandpa. I was excited for the possibility of escaping from this life, but honestly, I was scared to death that anything could go wrong.

On Friday after school, I came home and immediately went into the living room and sat on the floor next to Mom's lounge chair. I told her I had something to tell her. I spoke about the horrific abuse I had suffered at the hands of Henry, over the last eleven years in detail. She just sat still in her chair. There was no emotion or expression on her face. Once I was done, she asked me, "Why are you telling me this now? It happened such a long time ago!" I could see she had zero empathy or compassion for me or for what I had been through. It angered me, but at the same time, I wasn't surprised to hear such an uncaring, inappropriate statement from my mother. I had just shared that Henry had sexually abused me for years, and that he was the one who had broken my leg, among inflicting other forms of physical abuse on me. It really didn't seem to faze her. She acted as though she couldn't have cared less. Probably because she already knew. Horrible! I was speechless and it was obviously pointless to say anything else to her. I couldn't ever understand her thinking, but that was the end of the conversation, and the evening went forward. I had also completed what the counselor had asked me to do. One more step in the right direction toward freeing myself from this abusive home.

Henry came home from work Friday afternoon as usual. He took a shower and he and Mom got dressed up to go out for an expensive dinner, dancing, and cocktails. As usual, we kids had dinner at home, something frozen and cheap. The normal was frozen macaroni and cheese and applesauce. I never minded because they were out of the house, and we could have a peaceful night. It was actually a blessing. Later, I would be woken up in the early hours of the morning as they drove into the driveway and came walking into the house, usually around 2 a.m. As soon as I knew they were home, I would fall back asleep.

The next morning, as I was lying awake in my bed, I could hear Mom and Henry talking as they were lying in their bed, in their bedroom across the hall from mine. I couldn't hear everything that they were saying, but I believe Mom was telling Henry what I had just told her the day before about Henry sexually abusing me and breaking my leg. I was now scared to death and concerned about what he might do to me. I lay frozen in my bed, afraid to move. Before long I heard someone get out of their bed and walk toward my room. My heart was beating out of my chest as Henry walked into my room. He stood next to my bed, staring down at me as I lay completely still in my bed. A lot of unsaid words were being transmitted as he stared deeply into my eyes without moving or speaking. I wasn't sure what he was going to do to me. He looked angry. Eventually he spoke and said, "I am sorry for what I did to you and Cherie." I was shocked that those were the words that came out of his mouth, but I didn't feel he was truly sorry. I know those are the words he said, but I felt that he was threatening me with his voice and the stern look on his face. The message I was getting was...*I better not tell anyone else or he would handle this later, when no one was around!* I didn't trust him at all. Everything he did was calculated and in his best interest. I hadn't forgotten that for a minute. There wasn't any discussion about what he meant by saying sorry or what he was sorry about. He then said, "You aren't grounded any longer" and turned around and walked out of my room. I was shocked! I lay there for a minute collecting my thoughts. I knew that making it through the weekend would be easier now, since I wasn't grounded and could leave the house.

The weekend went by quickly. I was able to spend the night with my best friend. Monday afternoon was here before I knew it. I came home from school and quickly gathered my clothing and the items I planned on taking with me. I set them aside in an inconspicuous place in my bedroom. Then I went out to the living room and sat down on the floor next to Mom's lounge chair, where she was sitting. I told her that I was moving out today, that I was going to live with Grandpa and Grandma Byers, to get away from the abusive situation I was living in. I told her that Gram would be coming to pick me up by 4 p.m. She said, "No! you can't go! I am still your mother and in charge and you can't go!" Gram came, and my mother told her, "Judy isn't leaving!" Gram tried to say something to Mom, but it didn't work, and she refused to let me go. I could see that Gram was so overwhelmed by all of this and didn't know what to do. She got back into her car and left; she went back home without me.

Now I was really overwhelmed and scared. Gram had left without me, and I had opened a hornet's nest. Henry would be home soon, and I would be in so much trouble. I went back to my room and sat there.

Before long, Mom called out for me to come to the living room, where she was sitting in her lounge chair. She began to tell me that they "were" going to let me get a car next summer and a job. That I was going to miss out on all of that. She said if I still wanted to go, I could, but that I couldn't EVER come back home...NEVER!! I said, "I don't EVER want to come back here! I want to move out."

Surprisingly, Gram had come back to Mom's house and was sitting outside in her car. I would find out later that once she arrived home Grandpa asked, "Where is Judy?" She told him what had happened, and he said, "Get right back over there and get her!" That is why she returned to my house. Thank you, Grandpa!!! And Gram!! Praise God!

Gram wasn't allowed in the house, so I grabbed my stuff as quickly as I could and threw it in her car. I then said goodbye to my two younger siblings; they were about nine and ten years old. Sadly, they had no idea what was happening that day, and I couldn't tell them. It was the hardest part about moving out. I felt like I was leaving my own children behind.

Cherie wasn't home at the time, but was now an adult, so she could leave when she wanted to. I wasn't worried about Cherie's safety at home. She had turned eighteen years old but continued to live at home and pay rent to them. She came and went as she pleased. I ran out of the house, jumped on my ten-speed bicycle, and followed behind Gram's car. I was riding to my new life; this was really happening. I felt excited but also anxious and scared. As I rode away it felt like I was escaping, and I was. I had been enslaved to my mother and Henry for the past eleven years. Was I now free? I rode as fast as I could to my grandparents' home. I hoped that it was all over, but truthfully, I was scared to death that I might have to go back and live with Mom and Henry again.

Judy in front of Grandpa & Grandma Byers Mobile Home 1975

CHAPTER 16
BACK WITH GRAM & GRANDPA
Sixteen to Eighteen Years Old

G ram and I made it to their home safely that night. I moved in with Gram and Grandpa in the fall of 1974. At the time they lived in a two-bedroom mobile home in a beautiful park, which didn't allow anyone under fifty-five years old to live there. I had to be careful and quiet. I was just a "visitor" for a little over two years to the other seniors that lived there. But we made it work.

Later on, when I spoke to one of my younger siblings, I was told that when Henry came home that night after I moved out, he was extremely angry. He stated that it was good that he didn't catch me, or he would've "hung my ass out to dry." I knew he wouldn't be OK with me leaving and moving in with Grandpa and Grandma. For the first time in about eleven years, he wasn't in control of me or the situation.

When I moved in with my grandparents, I didn't know much about life or how to live out in the world. I hadn't really been exposed to much of the world. Living with Mom and Henry, I learned how to do housecleaning, care for my younger siblings, cook a little, ride my bike to the store and back to get some groceries, and do yardwork. They didn't spend any time talking to me about life, bills, earning a wage, people, relationships, college, religion, health, morals, love, service to humanity, or so many other important things I should know. Obviously, they wouldn't be able to teach me about many of those subjects I listed. It just wasn't in them. I would need to learn a lot about life in a short amount of time. Gram would help me.

Shortly after I moved out of the house, Cherie also moved out and into an apartment in town with her boyfriend. I would see them occasionally when they came by to visit at Gram and Grandpa's mobile home, and sometimes at church. They would help out by giving me a ride somewhere when I needed one. Cherie and her boyfriend got married in our church the following year. She asked me to be her maid of honor in the wedding, and I accepted.

It wasn't long before we developed a good routine around my grandparents' home. I was well taken care of and felt safe again. The mobile home we lived in had only two bedrooms. Gram and Grandpa each had their own bedroom before I moved in. Once I moved in with them, Gram gave me her room and her bed. She slept on the couch during the time I lived there. She wouldn't let it be any other way, you didn't tell her no! I couldn't talk her out of it. She was physically small, but strong in her decision-making and direction. Gram was so giving and put her family before herself. This is a perfect example. She was about seventy years old when she was sleeping on the couch, it breaks my heart.

It had to be difficult for them to raise a teenager, but they never showed it. They always made me feel loved and wanted. Grandpa was quiet and mainly in the background; he was the supportive grandfather that you knew was always there. He spent most of his time in a recliner watching television because of the pain associated with rheumatoid arthritis. It was difficult on a man who had been so active in his life. Gram was up and about, cooking, baking, washing, planting her garden or flowers, and helping to take care of Grandpa and me. I know that at her age, it was a struggle to find the energy needed to help raise a teenager. God bless them for taking me out of that situation. I now had hope and the desire to live.

During the two years while I lived with my grandparents, Gram often talked to me about life. She would tell me, "You have to be strong, and you have to move on, and you will make the right decisions." She gave me the knowledge that I should have received growing up. I was so blessed to have her and to teach me all that she did to prepare me for life. I can still hear her words today as I am doing something that she taught me, or when I am speaking to my children or grandchildren. I learned so many life lessons from her. She also pushed me to either go to college or into the military, where I could get an education.

Gram began building strength back into me. She would tell me that I had a good head on my shoulders and that she believed in me. She spoke so highly of me that it made me want to be what she thought I was. I remember thinking, "I'm not that good, but I want to be because of my love for her." I don't know if Gram had any idea how much good she was doing for me. She was building up a child who'd had the life taken out of her for the past eleven years. A child who had low self-esteem, no voice, and no sense of self. It made me want to do better and be better. It made me want to rise to the occasion. It made me care. I had lost a lot of the little bit of self that I had developed, before I went into the abusive situation. She pushed me to speak up for myself and to stand strong and know my value. Gram would say, "Just walk in the room like you own the place!" It would be a long time before I would be able to do that, if ever. As I became an adult, I knew I had to learn to find my voice. It was crucial for my well-being.

In Mom and Henry's house I had been suppressed and told that children were to be seen and not heard. I wasn't allowed to say anything. I learned don't speak or you will get injured, punched in the mouth, or slapped across the face. Sometimes kicked down the hall. I'm not speaking about being disrespectful, I am speaking about having a voice. I couldn't ever share my feelings or opinions, or correct something that wasn't true. I couldn't say I didn't like something (in a respectful way). I wasn't allowed to cry or show any emotion except one of acceptance for whatever they had said. No matter what they said, you were supposed to be like a robot and accept it with a smile on your face. I wasn't important, I just needed to shut up and do what I was told. I guess I failed at that, because I did cry "a lot" in my childhood, and as my mother would sarcastically say, "Judy just cries at the drop of a hat." I believe any child who has suffered the abuse that she allowed to happen to me, would have cried all the time too. I would get in trouble when I cried, but I couldn't stop the tears from coming.

It took me a long time to feel confident that I wasn't going to be sent back to live with my mother and stepfather. During the time I lived with Grandpa and Gram, I would have bad dreams that Henry and Mom had come and taken me back to their house. Back to the abusive situation. It was a nightmare that I couldn't shake because Henry had instilled so much fear in me. Thankfully that nightmare never came true. I never lived with Mom and Henry again, that hell was finally over.

I graduated from high school in June of 1976. Two months later, Aunt Merikay, Uncle Butch, and their two daughters also moved to Hemet, California. They stayed with us for about a month, until they found their own place. Sadly, Grandpa died September 6, 1976, only a few months after I graduated. Gram and I were with him in his hospital room when he passed. That day I witnessed her deep sorrow and pain as she lost her longtime husband and friend. It was extremely sad.

I was getting close to turning eighteen years old and becoming an adult, when I received a call from Mom. I hadn't heard from her since I left home, and nearly two years had gone by. She wanted me to meet her at a restaurant in town so she could give me my birthday gift. I reluctantly agreed, and we set up a time.

When she showed up, she had my two younger siblings with her, and that was a nice surprise. They were happy to see me and were all smiles. I was glad to see them too and it made it a happier event. Mom gave me a two-piece set of bright-orange luggage and a birthday card. We all got brownie sundaes, and mine had a lit candle on it. Mom also asked the waiter to sing Happy Birthday to me. I felt embarrassed, this was all so odd. I was uncomfortable sitting in the restaurant with Mom, who was acting like everything was normal. Especially since our last real conversation was almost two years ago, where I told her how Henry severely abused me throughout my childhood. Her behavior that day was even more confirmation for me that she knew all along what he had done to me.

I shouldn't have agreed to meet with her, it was a mistake. She had just gone on in life having checked Cherie and Judy off the list and only two more children to go until they were all out of her house. I should have known that nothing had changed, but I ignorantly had the hope that she would wake up and do the right thing for her children and herself. Henry should have been out of that house immediately, and she should have divorced him.

But she chose him and all the "stuff," the material things, once again. Of course, her motive was to get me to forget the past and just go forward. To never look back or talk about it again. That would greatly benefit her life. A quick and cheap eighteenth birthday celebration and some ugly bright-orange suitcases that were probably on clearance, would fix everything. I wasn't ever motivated by material things. I can't imagine how she thought it could all just be forgotten, washed under the rug. She was still the same person I had known my whole life; it was all about her. We exchanged some small talk and in about an hour it was over and time to go. I loved seeing my siblings, but I couldn't get away from her quick enough. It was painful to engage with her, knowing she hadn't done anything about what Henry had done to me. I think this was the final celebration for her; it was the ending of any obligation to her unwanted daughter, Judy.

I left the restaurant and returned home to be with my Gram. Over the years she and I would share many eye-opening stories about Mom, just trying to make sense of something that you couldn't make sense of. We were trying to come to terms with Mom's bad decisions, and the aftermath of those bad decisions that we both had to live with. The following is one of the difficult stories Gram shared about Mom.

After Mom graduated from high school, she wanted to go to college in Wisconsin to study biology. Gram and Grandpa were supportive of this and moved her up there, helped her to enroll, and paid for her to live in a room that was rented out to college students. Soon after they returned home to Illinois, they tried calling her many times, and never got an answer. Not being able to reach her, they got worried and contacted the woman who they rented the room from. She told them that soon after Mom moved in, a man Mom knew from her hometown had come up there, and she left with him. The woman hadn't seen Mom since.

Gram and Grandpa were shocked and upset. They knew who this man was, and he wasn't anyone they would want their daughter to be around. He was known as the town bum. They were worried sick because now they had no idea where Mom was. Gram faithfully left the porch light on every night, hoping

Mom would come home, but they didn't hear a word from her. A year later they got a call from some good friends of theirs who said Mom had showed up at their home, alone, and didn't have any of her belongings with her. She told them she was afraid to call home because they would be mad at her. Gram and Grandpa were happy that she was alive and safe, but also embarrassed because she went to their friends' home as though she couldn't go to her own home. Mom had a manipulative way of becoming the victim and turning the blame and focus on someone else instead of herself. She wasn't accountable for her actions, and she had continued this pattern throughout her life.

It was always very painful for Gram to think that her daughter treated her children the way she did. She would tearfully, and with a tone of anger, say, "I didn't raise her that way!" Gram just couldn't comprehend her thinking or behavior. I couldn't either. I would tell Gram to just forget about her, to just let her go.

CHAPTER 17

BEGINNING MY LIFE AS AN ADULT

Eighteen Years Old

When I became an adult and went out into the world on my own, I had no idea how much the child abuse and trauma would continue to have a direct impact on my life. It wasn't a topic that was spoken about, like it is today. If I brought the subject up to different adult family members in my life, I was told not to talk about it, and asked, "Why would you want to talk about something so negative?" At that time, the general thinking of how to handle any form of child abuse and trauma, was to just go forward and put it all behind you, and that is what I tried to do.

I moved into a rental house with my best friend's older brother, who was already living there. He needed a roommate to help pay expenses and offered me this opportunity. It was sad for both Gram and me when I moved out of her home, but I felt like it was time for me to make my own way in the world. Gram would now be living alone for the first time in over fifty years. It would be a big adjustment for her.

I was young and naive, having no idea what it would take to support myself, especially without any specialized training or education. I got a full-time job working at a factory that was about a block from my home. I only lasted a few weeks. The job was very boring, and I had trouble staying awake. We started at 7 a.m. sharp, no talking, just sitting at a long table with each of us doing something to small parts that took a few seconds, and then you would grab another one and do it again, and again. The whistle blew at 9 a.m. for break time. At this point I would go straight to the bathroom and splash cold water on my face to wake up. After fifteen minutes the whistle blew again, and you were back sitting at the table doing the same thing until the lunch whistle blew at 11:30 a.m. Then you would eat lunch and in a half-hour, return to the table. Ugh! I tried working at another factory nearby and it wasn't much different, I lasted about a month. During the time I lived with Gram and Grandpa, I had a few different jobs in food service, and one job working as a retail clerk, but they were only part-time jobs and now I needed a full-time job to be able to pay my bills.

Gram gave me her old car under the condition that I would enroll in the community junior college and take a few classes. I wasn't ready to commit to college at the time, but I agreed anyway. I was interested in becoming a juvenile probation officer, so I took classes in criminal law. I wanted to be able to help troubled children. Now that I had a car, I could also find full-time employment.

I was determined that my adult life would be entirely different from my childhood. I often daydreamed as a child about how good my life would be as an adult. I knew that one day I would be in a healthy and loving relationship with a wonderful man. The abuse I had suffered didn't destroy my ability to have a physically intimate and emotional relationship. I was very fortunate to be able to distinctly separate the difference. I always wanted to have my own happy family and I knew it could be possible.

One area in my life that was deeply affected by my childhood was trust. It was difficult for me to trust, and I only had a guarded level of it with anyone, in any relationship, with the exception of Gram. I completely trusted Gram.

Brian was now my steady boyfriend; I had been dating him off and on since I was sixteen years old. I had a level of trust for him, and that was the most that I could offer him at that time in my life. I was used to being very guarded, not trusting people, it was safer for me and my method of survival. Brian was fun and nice to me, and we were connected. Over time we had fallen in love with each other. But he also had done things that had broken my trust. Even so, I continued on in the relationship. I didn't want to give up on love and a family.

I also developed a close relationship with Brian's family, especially his mother. Every time I saw her, she would kiss me and tell me she loved me. This was so different for me; my own mother never kissed me or told me that she loved me. His mother always made me feel loved and that she cared about me. Our relationship grew, and I could tell her anything. She never judged me, but always tried to help in any way she could. I was developing a deep trust with her. I realized years later, I stayed in the dysfunctional relationship I was in with Brian at the time because I never wanted to lose the loving relationships I had with his family.

After a few months of living at the rental house, my roommate moved out and in with his girlfriend, and then Brian moved in with me. We both loved animals, so we added a white and beige puppy to our home that we named "Misty." She was a Samoyed and German Shepard mix, and the veterinarian told me she had coyote in her as well. Misty was a good dog and companion for us. I loved having a dog again.

During this time Cherie and her husband moved to Washington state, where some of her husband's family lived. She was a few states away from where I lived, so we didn't see each other for quite a while. At this point I could barely afford to pay my bills; I definitely couldn't afford to go visit her in another state. Financially she was at the same point, struggling to get settled. We would visit with each other on the phone when we could. She was living her life and I was living mine. We were both trying to get our lives going in a positive direction. Our sister relationship was ok, but we weren't really close.

Six months later Brian and I left that rental house and moved into our own rental apartment. We moved to an older two-story rental house that had been converted into two separate apartments. One on the top floor and one on the bottom floor. We had the bottom apartment. The building was on the side of a hill with a view. The owner of the apartments grew Christmas trees on his acreage, which ran below the apartments. As a part of the monthly rental payment, we watered his Christmas trees. Money was tight, so that was helpful.

There were always ups and downs in our relationship, each of us had our own baggage, our own unresolved issues that would rise up every now and then. We were young and trying to make our way in the world.

CHAPTER 18
MY BROTHER COMES TO LIVE WITH US
Nineteen Years Old

I had recently started a new job and was at work the morning I got a call from my mother. I was startled to hear from her because we hadn't spoken in a year. She said she had caught my thirteen-year-old brother smoking cigarettes and that she couldn't handle him any longer and wondered if I wanted him. What? of course I wanted him! WOW! I immediately said, "YES!" But I told her that I would have to wait until I got off work at 5 p.m. to get him. I was working at a new job, and I couldn't just leave. She asked if I could get him at lunch time instead and I agreed.

My brother and I had a close relationship while we were growing up, and we remained in close contact after I moved in with our grandparents. On a few rare occasions, Mom and Henry allowed him to come over and visit me. After I became an adult and moved out on my own, I would find ways to be able to meet up with him, without Mom and Henry knowing it. One time when he had a school event in the evening, I went there to be able to see him. Mom and Henry never went to these events, so it was perfect. Sometimes I would pick him up from school instead of him riding the bus home. That way we would have about forty-five minutes to spend together before he was due home. After we visited, I would drop him off at his bus stop at the same time that the school bus normally did. He would walk home from there, arriving home at his regular time. It all worked out and Mom and Henry never knew we were spending time together. I was more like a parent to him than a sister. I worried about him being at the house without me; I could see he was struggling with that change. It was a normal transition for my brother to come and live with me, rather than Cherie. She also lived in another state at the time.

I wasn't sure why Mom was in such a rush to move my brother out of the house, or to give him to me. It was strange that she was even offering my brother to me. What did that mean? She had favored him his whole childhood, he was her only son and Henry was his biological father. It didn't add up. I never, ever, thought the day would come when they would give him up, or let him come and live with ME. This act was nothing short of a miracle; it had to be a Divine intervention, and I was grateful.

At noon I left work to pick up my brother and bring him to my home. I went down the elevator and out the door to the parking lot, where I was surprised to see that he was sitting in the passenger's side of my car. I could see he had been crying and looked distraught. My car had also been loaded with all of his personal belongings. I wondered why my mother couldn't even wait a few hours until I could pick him up. She had just dropped him off and shoved all of his stuff in my car. Mom was gone, leaving him sitting there alone. I felt sorry for my brother, having to go through this rejection at such a young age. I quickly drove him to my home, dropped him off, and then returned to work. I hated to have to leave him, but I needed to keep my new job. My head was spinning with all the changes this would mean, but I loved my brother and would do anything to help him.

The following day I got a call from my mother. She wanted my brother back home. I refused. He didn't want to go back, nor would going back be in his best interest. There was no way I was going to send him back if I could do anything to help him. Over the following week, my mother would randomly call and demand that he come back home. I always said, "NO! He is going to stay here, living with me and Brian.

Gram was supportive of my brother living with us and suggested that I get legal advice, which she offered to pay for. I met with an attorney who advised me of my legal rights and what to do to retain my brother in our home. I learned that the longer he was living with us and we were caring for him, the stronger the case would be to keep him in our home. He continued living with us, and we knew that every day was one step closer to us keeping him.

At one point, probably out of desperation, my mother spoke to the youth authorities, telling them that she wanted my brother to return home to live with her and Henry again. She told them that he was living with me, and that I wouldn't bring him back home. They contacted me and asked that I come in for a meeting. I met with them and explained how I had obtained my brother, and about the abusive childhood I had lived through under Mom and Henry's care. They informed me that my mother had spoken badly about me, but after meeting with me, they saw that I was responsible and was nothing like she had said I was. They weren't concerned and stated that they didn't plan to do anything to return him to her home.

I continued getting random phone calls from my mother, she was trying different approaches to get my brother back. These calls would always upset my brother and he would worry that he could be taken back home. I knew my brother needed this emotional roller coaster to end, and I knew he would be better living with us. So, the next call I got from my mother, I told her he was going to stay with me and if she didn't stop calling, I would be forced to tell people at Henry's place of employment how he abused me, and what kind of man he really was. I never got another call from her. This was more validation that she knew what the truth was, and she didn't want it to be revealed.

Life went forward and all was going pretty well. We moved into a duplex closer to town where my brother could have his own bedroom. He seemed happy living with us and had close friends who came over often and would stay at our home. Brian and my brother got along well, and he was supportive of him living with us. Brian's family was also very welcoming of my brother.

Cherie had been living in the state of Washington for about four years now. She was employed as a Certified Nursing Assistant while she attended college from 1977 through 1979. She completed the nursing program and became a Licensed Practical Nurse (LPN) when she was twenty-three years old. We hadn't seen much of each other during that time, but we continued to keep in contact by phone.

Brian and I got married in April of 1980 on the lawn of the church I attended as a child and that had provided a place of safety for me. My brother was now fifteen years old and was a groomsman in our wedding. Gram was very involved, somewhere in between the "mother of the bride" and "grandmother of the bride." Aunt Merikay helped out and Uncle Butch walked me down the aisle to give me away. Cherie flew down from Washington to be my matron of honor. My cousin Cynde and my sister-in-law (to be) Vonneta were my bridesmaids, along with a girl friend of mine. Both sides of the family were there in support, with the exception of my mother and Henry, who of course weren't invited.

A few months later, our brother went to visit with Cherie and her husband in Washington, during the summer while he was out of school. Then in the fall, Cherie came down for a week to stay with me when my first child was due. I gave birth the day after Cherie arrived, to my beautiful daughter who was born on my brother's sixteenth birthday. It was really special that it worked out that way. My daughter and my brother quickly became close. She loved her uncle, and he adored his niece. Their relationship touched my heart and brought more joy and happiness to our home, helping to create a deeper bond within our family. Cherie's timely arrival was perfect. We got to spend time together with the new baby before she had to return home. My Gram just loved that baby and spent a lot of time teaching me how to care for her.

Brian's mother and father had been divorced for many years before I met them. Their relationship was strained and pretty much nonexistent. But when I became pregnant with our first child, his mother decided it was time to move forward and let go of the past. She contacted Brian's father and explained that since they were going to be grandparents who would both like to spend time together with the family, it would be in everyone's best interest to let go of any differences they had between them. He agreed, and because of that, we had so many happy and loving times together. I admired both of them for choosing this path.

Shortly after our daughter was born, we moved into a large rental house so she could have her own bedroom. It had a large front yard and backyard, so there was more space for everybody. Brian's father, who lived out of town, would come and spend weekends with us. He was so excited about having his first grandchild. I spent a lot of time with Brian's father, and we became close. It was wonderful to see how much he loved our daughter. He found so much joy in her just being a child. Brian's mother was wonderful also. We were already close, and she loved her granddaughter. She would help in any way she could, and I always knew I could go to her for any help I needed.

In the spring of 1981, Cherie gave birth to her first child, a beautiful daughter. She was born on Cherie's twenty-fifth birthday! When the baby was a few months old, Gram sent Cherie the money for an airplane ticket to fly out for a visit with all of us. We all wanted to meet the new baby girl. Cherie stayed at our home and never went back to Washington. She wasn't happy in her marriage and had decided to get a divorce. I fully supported her decisions. Soon, she got a job at the local hospital, and after a few months Cherie and her daughter moved into their own apartment in Hemet. Shortly after moving into the apartment, Cherie began a new relationship and they moved into a rental home together.

Life continued on and my brother finished driver's education and got his driver's license and a vehicle. He began working part-time to earn enough money to pay for gas and insurance. We didn't have a lot, but we had each other, including our Gram, who was always involved in our lives, helping as she could. We had many family get-togethers at that house, making a lot of good memories.

CHAPTER 19
MY YOUNGER SISTER COMES TO LIVE WITH US
Twenty-Three Years Old

Four years after my brother moved in with us, I was contacted by my younger sister, who at the time was sixteen years old. She also wanted to move in with us. She was the last child living at home with Mom and Henry. They weren't abusing her, but she wanted to get away from the depressing home life she was living. Once our brother had moved out, there were lots of changes in the home, including Mom not wanting to celebrate Christmas anymore. Our younger sister felt that her presence in the house was insignificant to Mom and Henry. She had always felt closer to me than Cherie, so she asked if she could come and live with me and my family.

Our brother was now seventeen years old and would be graduating from high school within a year. We welcomed our sister's desire to live with us and created a plan to make it happen.

We believed that Mom or Henry might put up a struggle, but we knew that legally, our sister could make this choice for herself if she had a safe place to live.

We set up a date and a plan to get her out of their house in a way that would avoid any confrontation with Mom or Henry. On that day, she got ready for school in the morning and walked to her bus stop as though it was a normal day, but she didn't get on the bus. Mom and Henry went to work and after the bus left, she quickly returned home to the now empty house. We were waiting close by and drove over to the house when we figured she had returned home. We quickly loaded up all of her clothes and personal belongings. As she was leaving the house for the last time, she left Mom and Henry a note on the table stating that she had moved out and was moving in with us.

Our sister didn't have her driver's license yet, but Mom and Henry had bought her a car because she would be getting it soon. Henry was driving her car back and forth to work each day, so that morning it was sitting down at his place of employment. She wanted to have her car and she had the keys to it, so we went by and got it. Brian drove it to our house and put it in our garage. I knew this part wouldn't go over well. But I thought it was worth a try because she would need a car, and they had purchased that one for her.

Unfortunately, I was right. The police showed up at our home early the next morning. They said Mom and Henry had filed a report that our sixteen-year-old sister had left them to live with us, and that she had taken her car with her. The police wanted us to meet them down at the station in an hour, which we did. This was the first time I was going to be in the same room with Henry since I had moved out seven years ago, and he still terrified me. It triggered a post-traumatic stress reaction in me. I knew he would be extremely angry about everything that we had done.

As requested, we all met at the police station that morning. Henry walked into the room and even though he was wearing dark sunglasses, I could still see the rage on his face. He sat at the end of the table and gave off a very visible furious energy. The rest of us sat at the same large table, including the police officers. We discussed our younger sister moving in with us along with taking the vehicle. I advised the police that we had lived in an abusive situation at home with Mom and Henry, and that is why I left at sixteen years old. This didn't seem to faze the police officers, and no follow-up questions were asked. It seems so strange that they didn't do anything about the child abuse accusations, but that's how it was in 1981!

It wasn't long before it was obvious that all Mom and Henry wanted back was the gift they'd given to my sister, the car. It was always about the money for Mom. We agreed to return the car. Our younger sister could stay with us, which is what we wanted all along, so it worked out. The meeting ended with the police officers saying, "You know, it's almost Thanksgiving and all of you should let go of the past and have a big family get-together on Thanksgiving." Huh?! Did I hear that right? We'd just told the officers about the child abuse that we suffered under Mom and Henry's roof and now they thought everything could just be swept under the rug?! I walked out of there with my head spinning.

Even so, it was wonderful and a relief to have my youngest sibling back in my life and living with me. She was helpful and fun and fit right into our family. Brian's family was welcoming of her as well. We were becoming a big, close extended family. She was a teenager now, and I was getting to know her as the beautiful young lady she was becoming. We had many long and informative talks about our abusive and dysfunctional childhood. I would learn that Henry never sexually abused her. I thank God she was spared from that horrific trauma. At times, he did physically abuse her. When he was angry, he would grab her quickly by the arm or somewhere on her body, or by her clothing, and throw her across the room. She also witnessed our brother being physically abused, which was traumatic for her. It was traumatic for all of us when another one of us was getting abused.

About a week or so after the meeting at the police station, Mom called and said she wanted to come over and visit with us. She wanted to spend some time with us. I said OK and we set up a time for her to come. The thought of it made me uncomfortable, but I was trying to be open for my younger siblings and also for myself. I think for a brief moment, I still had an unrealistic hope that she could change or become the mother she never was.

The day she came over it was just me, my younger sister, and my year-old daughter at the house. My brother knew she was coming but didn't stay home to visit with her. The first thing she said was, "Where is your brother?" She looked around for him, missing the fact that her one-year-old granddaughter who she'd never met was sitting right in front of her, along with her youngest daughter and me. We could see she had only come to see our brother. Yet again, she was only interested in him and not us. I quickly snapped right back into reality. This was her first visit to my home, and it would be her last. That was the final day for me with her. I saw her exactly as she was and would go forward in my life without her.

It gave me a deep sense of peace that none of my siblings were living with Mom and Henry any longer. I wouldn't have ever guessed that it could turn out that way, that it was even possible that both of my younger siblings would be living with me before they were adults.

Our brother graduated from high school in 1982 and lived with us for another year. He then moved in with Cherie and her family for a few months in their home in Hemet. He joined the California Conservation Corps and moved to their location in Northern California. While he was gone, we kept in close contact through letters and phone calls.

Our youngest sister graduated from high school in 1983. She quickly found employment and moved out on her own in Hemet. A few years later, without my knowledge at the time, she went to Henry's place of employment and confronted him about the horrible child abuse he inflicted on Cherie and me. He tried to deflect what she was saying by talking negatively about her and her life. She stood strong and continued with what she had set out to do. She was so strong that day, he didn't have any power over her.

She then came over and told me what she had done. I was truly shocked and scared for her, but I also admired her strength.

Standing up to Henry for us was so strong and honorable. She told me she did it because she loved me and that I was like a mother to her, and she knew I couldn't do it. She said she would do anything for me. It was difficult for her to think of us as being hurt. Even though she wasn't born yet, or she was too young to know what was happening to us, she has always believed Cherie and me.

CHAPTER 20
A NEW LIFE AND AN ENDING OF AN OLD ONE

U p to this point in my adult life, I was always pushing forward, doing what needed to be done, while suppressing my emotions. I lived with an underlying feeling of sadness, a heaviness in my body that would fluctuate in intensity. Some days I would feel anger, and my physical body would feel tight and full of pressure. Other days I just didn't feel well. In my mid-twenties I went into counseling to get guidance on how to work through problems that we were having in my first marriage. Each attempt at counseling became a financial hardship, so I couldn't continue to go after a few sessions. At that time in my life, and because of what I had been told, my thinking was that the child abuse was something that had happened to me years ago, when I was a child, and that it was behind me.

In 1984, I gave birth to my second child, a handsome and healthy son. Over the past year my marriage had been falling apart. We had separated and then gotten back together right before the baby was born. Months later we separated again, and Brian moved up to Yucca Valley, California. He found employment up there and was staying with friends. We reconciled once again and the two children and I moved up to Yucca Valley in 1985 to start a new life together. It was difficult to move away from Gram and both of our families in Hemet, but I felt it was important to try to make the marriage work, especially with two young children. It was about an hour-and-twenty-minute drive to go back and visit them. I went as often as I could, especially to see Gram.

A couple of weeks after we moved to Yucca Valley, the kids and I had to return to Hemet, because I had previously been scheduled for a major surgery. We stayed at Cherie's house as I went through the surgery and recovery. Brian would come to stay and help out on the weekends, and other days when he didn't have to work. Cherie and other family members helped with caring for the children until I was well enough to do it myself. After about a month, the kids and I returned to Yucca Valley to stay.

About a month later, I was able to find full-time employment that lasted for approximately six months. When that job ended, I enrolled in the junior college and began working toward a degree in business. After struggling financially for years, I was now motivated to attend college. I should have listened to Gram initially, but I didn't. At twenty-six years old, and with two children to support, and in an unstable marriage, I was finally at the place in my life where I was willing to commit to a college education.

At the end of the summer of 1985, Cherie married her second husband, and became a blended family with her daughter and his three young children. She then returned to college to continue her education in nursing, while she also worked full-time. In December of 1986, she received her associate degree in nursing, and became a Registered Nurse. She continued working full-time. Cherie's life was so busy that there wasn't any time to focus on herself or address the ongoing abuse and the effects it was having on her decisions and life choices.

Our brother had left the "CCC" and was living with us again and working in town. Our younger sister had recently given birth to her first child, and she was excited to be a mother.

I initially went to college full-time, taking courses that offered office skills, just in case I had to return to work. We bought a home and moved to Joshua Tree, California in 1987. My brother moved with us, but only for a short time before he moved into his own place. After going to college full-time for a year and a half, I had to find employment to help with the finances. The new skills were an asset, and I found full-time employment. I continued to go to college part-time in the evenings, working toward the business degree.

In early 1990, I knew I wasn't "in love" with Brian any longer. Throughout our relationship we had been through some very difficult times. Brian had been both physically and emotionally abusive to me. His years of substance abuse had damaged our relationship in ways that were irreparable. It changed the way I felt about him. Sometimes people's actions drain the love right out of you, and you can't get it back. There were many times I should have ended our relationship because of his destructive behavior, but I didn't. I wasn't strong enough to make the right decision. At this point we were just continuing to go along in life, raising our children, and staying together. It had become a marriage of convenience, instead of one of love.

When I told Brian how I felt, he asked me to give him six more months to make things better, which I agreed to. I had been through this with him many times before, and I knew this would be the last time I would be willing to give him another chance. I felt it was important to know that I had done everything to try to keep our marriage together, especially because of our children.

At the end of the six months, I became physically ill. I believe it was because I knew the marriage was over, and the illness was the final purge of this dysfunctional relationship. I also knew that this time I had to make the right decision for myself and my children. I couldn't sidestep this any longer. Making this change would be another step forward in the journey of healing myself. In the end it taught me that I could choose how I wanted to live my life. That I was the one responsible to take those steps to a better life, and that I was capable.

In November of 1990, I told Brian I wanted a divorce. I was fearful of how this discussion would go, but deep down inside he already knew. He was sad, but calm about it all. We decided to continue living together through the holidays and until we finished the college class we were taking together. In January of 1991 we sat the children down and told them we were getting a divorce. They both cried, and we cried too. It was difficult for a six- and ten-year-old to understand. Brian moved out a couple weeks later. I filed the papers, he signed them in agreement, and we were divorced in 1991.

CHAPTER 21
LOVE

I met Steve after I moved up to Yucca Valley, where he was currently living. We were friends for many years and our friendship grew into love. He was kind, loving, humble, compassionate, intelligent, and ambitious. He was also handsome, fun, a good provider, and a good father; he had two children of his own. The relationship with Steve was so different from anything I had ever experienced. There were times where I thought, "This is too good to be true." I was waiting for the other shoe to drop, but it never did. The relationship just got better, and the love we felt for each other got deeper.

Until this point in my life, Ole Gram was the only person who I had a shared a deep loving relationship with my entire life. She was getting older, and I truly feared her death. I feared losing that love and connection. I could always go to her and know I would be loved and comforted; she always had my best interest at heart. Gram's unconditional love validated me, helping me with my self-worth during times when I often felt like nothing. Her love helped me to have love for myself. Everyone needs at least one person who loves them unconditionally, someone who is always there for you. For me, that was my Gram.

As my relationship with Steve continued to grow, I was slowly releasing my fear of losing Gram. I was now in a stable, loving, and committed relationship. There was a sense of peace between us I hadn't experienced before. It was wonderful. I knew Steve loved me, I knew he was committed to our relationship and our family. I knew I could count on him for anything. He continued to prove that to me daily.

On March 16th of 1992, I got a call from Aunt Merikay. Ole Gram had passed, and I needed to go to Hemet right away. Steve was out of town, so I dropped the kids off with a friend of mine and then drove down to Gram's home. She was still lying peacefully on her bed when I got there. I was able to sit with her for a while before the coroner came to take her body away.

Later that night, when Steve got home and found out Gram had passed away, he got right back in his truck and drove down to Hemet to comfort me and spend the night with me at Aunt Merikay and Uncle Butch's home. I don't think I have ever cried so hard in my life. It was a shock for Steve to see me that way. He stayed the following day to help at Gram's, and then he went home later that afternoon to care for our four children. When I came home a day later, he had dinner cooking on the stove. He was using one of Gram's vegetable steamers that he had brought home from her kitchen. It was such a heartfelt way to comfort me.

Our love continued to grow, and in June of 1993, Steve and I were married in a beautiful outdoor setting, with our children, families, and friends surrounding us. We were in love and very happy to be together.

Life went forward with both of us working full-time and raising our children. I continued to go to college part-time in the evenings. In June of 1994, I graduated, earning an associate degree in business. Aunt Merikay and Uncle Butch along with Steve and our children, and my younger sister were there to support me. Ole Gram would have been smiling down on me that day.

CHAPTER 22
MOMENTS OF AWARENESS AND INSIGHT
Counseling

I n my mid-forties, I was experiencing undiagnosed health problems. I was looking at everything that could possibly be the cause. My children were adults now and I had more time to focus on myself and my own life. I was questioning if my childhood trauma was impacting my physical health, so I began professional counseling with John, to rule that out. Subsequently, I found that the abuse wasn't what was causing that medical condition, but it was causing other physical and emotional manifestations. Counseling was an awakening for me. I was clearly able to see the effects that the abuse and trauma had on my life. I knew this could be beneficial for Cherie too, and I asked if she wanted to join me. She did.

Joint counseling was a turning point in our relationship as we each opened up and shared our truth about the abuse that we had each experienced in our childhood. This was a healing and informative time for us. We both discovered things that we didn't know about each other, or about the childhood abuse that each of us had suffered. This is when Cherie learned that I was being sexually abused as well, and that it continued happening to me long after it stopped for her. She had no idea I was being sexually abused and I was completely shocked to find this out over thirty-five years later.

From that one moment in my childhood, when I was about eight years old, sitting in the car, watching Cherie and Mom talk as they stood in front of a store, I had believed that during their talk, Cherie had told our mother that I was also being sexually abused. She hadn't.

In counseling, Cherie confirmed that on that day in front of the store, she had told Mom she was being sexually abused, but Mom didn't believe her. Mom said something to the effect of… Oh, no-no… this couldn't be happening. Cherie also said that she told Mom that only she was being sexually abused, because at that time, Cherie didn't know that I was also being sexually abused by Henry. All along she thought that it was only HER, and that it was resolved after she spoke with Mom because Henry never sexually abused her again.

As I think about it now, I can see why Cherie didn't know I was being sexually abused, because she wasn't ever at home when it happened to me. She was usually gone with Mom or over at a friend's house. On the other hand, the reason I knew Cherie was being sexually assaulted by Henry, is because I had been at home some of the times when it happened. I was locked outside and heard her crying and knew what was happening because it had happened to me. In counseling Cherie also learned the full extent of the abuse and torture I suffered as a child. At that point, Cherie and her family ended any contact with Mom and Henry forever.

We both learned in counseling that in-home sexual predators must divide and isolate their victims to protect themselves from being caught. They keep the children from forming an alliance. Henry knew that for him to have control over each of us, he would have to destroy our close bond and create a separate bond with Cherie. He would build her alliance to him and turn her against me. As a perpetrator, he couldn't risk the forming of a sibling coalition because it could be his downfall. Henry had definitely accomplished his goal; Cherie and I weren't close for decades before we finally bonded again.

All four of us siblings grew up with so many negative messages from Mom and Henry. When Cherie and I discuss why Mom treated me like she did, we believe it stemmed from her associating me with her divorce, which represented failure to her. In the distorted way Mom looked at life, her pregnancy with me made her life fall apart. As Cherie put it, "Judy was the fault of everything," and I believe Cherie was right, because I constantly felt that way. I was always blamed for everything and punished for it all too. When Cherie was born, her father was in the home, and they were still married. When I was born there wasn't a father, "a man" in her life. She was living on the farm with her parents, which she hated. When my younger brother and sister were born, Mom was married to their father, and he was in the home. Is that the answer to why Mom had such disdain toward me? I don't think I will ever know for sure.

Each time I discuss this with Cherie or read to her the horrific truth I have just written in this book, I learn a little bit more about Cherie. This time she shared that when she was being sexually abused, she was also forced to have oral sex with Henry. She said that at the time this was happening, Henry threatened her by telling her that he would kill all of us if she told anyone about the sexual abuse. This was the first time Cherie shared this with me, and even though I know how enraged and violent Henry could become, it is still shocking. I also have suppressed memories from my childhood come forward from time to time.

Our counselor told us that because of our horrific childhood we could have become monsters, prostitutes, drug addicts, horrible mothers, or landed in prison; but we didn't. We are caring and compassionate women who are loving parents and grandparents, who earned college degrees and became strong, functioning women in society. Our childhood was an example of what we didn't want in our adult lives.

The time we spent together in counseling was extremely valuable and life changing for both of us. We learned that we had coped with sexual abuse differently. Over time I learned so much about child abuse, trauma, myself, and Cherie. It truly began the road of healing and brought a sense of freedom. Our professional counselor was compassionate, validating, and highly skilled in child abuse and trauma. He provided a safe and compassionate space to open up and truthfully share the horrific stories of our past. He validated our feelings and emotions while guiding us to understand that those feelings were normal because of what we had been through. Each joint counseling session brought awareness, healing, and acceptance of self. As adults, Cherie and I would spend time together, but I don't think we were ever as close as we are today. The joint counseling helped us to better understand each other now, and when we were children. These sessions continued for eighteen months, until Cherie moved out of state.

Counseling has also helped me to see those who abused me for who they really are. Mentally ill? Victims of child abuse and/ or trauma themselves? Somewhere in those areas probably lies the answer. I believe that for society to be effective in ending the horrific acts that one person does to another, it is necessary to get to the root of the problem. What are the individual core stories of the perpetrators, bullies, sexual offenders, child abusers, violent offenders, sex traffickers, rapists, and murderers of our world? Is it because of a mental health condition? Did childhood trauma affect brain development? Is addiction playing a part in their behavior? Or maybe something horribly traumatic happened in their life? Did something happen that has changed them to become monsters? Many criminals/perpetrators were severely damaged by the abuse and trauma they suffered as a child. In turn they go out into the world and become violent offenders themselves.

Why do some people go through horrific child abuse and trauma, and turn out to be competent and loving adults? Then others become perpetrators, criminals, violent offenders, addicts, or any other form of a dysfunctional adult? I believe it has to do with the type of relationships with adults you had as a child, and the influence it had on your life. Did you have someone who loved you unconditionally? Someone who was supportive and always there for you? Someone who always had your best interest at heart? Love is so powerful.

In the end we both made it through this and have risen well above it. Cherie is a loving, compassionate, and caring person who would help anyone. Her chosen profession as a Registered Nurse, and as a Hospice Nurse, was truly her calling. One of her coworkers shared with me that she was an amazing nurse who could quickly develop intimate relationships with her dying patients. Because she is open, authentic, and non-judgmental, her patients loved her and often felt safe enough to share something that they had been holding on to, which in turn allowed them to let go and depart this life in peace. Cherie is a beautiful example of striving to move beyond the past and giving the world her best. She continues to walk forward in life using all her resources and inner strength to carry her to her best days. I love my older sister and am so proud of her.

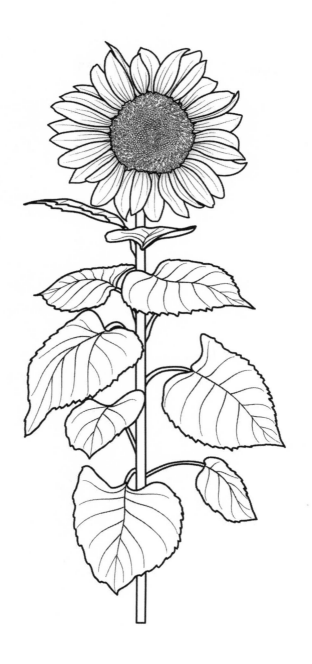

Grandma Marie and Grandpa John Mc Namara

CHAPTER 23
A WORD ON THE MAN WHO WAS MY BIOLOGICAL FATHER
The Paternal Side of Our Family

John and Marie McNamara, our paternal grandparents, had one son, David William McNamara, our biological father, born on March 13, 1927, in Sycamore, Illinois. He was their only child, as he was born in the middle of the Great Depression. They never felt like they could afford more children until they were both too old.

Our father, David, left high school when he was seventeen and joined the Marines. He wasn't doing his schoolwork at the time and some of his friends were enlisting, so our grandparents signed the papers to allow him to also enlist. He was in the Marines for a few years, including being in combat (World War II) and going to China. I believe that this is how he ended up living in the Florida Keys.

Grandma Marie said that our Father's first marriage was to a "good woman" for a brief period of time. They

177

divorced because he was just too young. They didn't have any children together.

Our father would make trips from Florida back home to Sycamore, Illinois to visit family and friends. It was during one of those trips that he met our mother at a bar in town. In time, she decided to move to Florida to be with him. Grandma Marie tried talking her out of going, telling her that David was still not ready to settle down, but she went anyway.

Our mother and father were married in 1955 in Coral Gables, Florida and made their home in Key Largo, Florida. Cherie was born the following spring, the first-born child to both parents. In the summer of 1958, our mother and father's relationship was deteriorating, so our father put both our mother, who was seven months pregnant with me, and Cherie, just two and a half years old, on a plane to Sycamore, Illinois to live with Mom's parents. Our father came to Illinois shortly before I was born to see if there was any possibility of reconciliation, but there wasn't, and he went back to Florida to live.

I was born about a month after our father left. He wasn't present for my birth …he never called or came to meet me…he wasn't a part of my childhood at all. I had never seen his face in a picture or otherwise. I didn't know if he was dead or alive or if I had a father, and Mom never talked to us about him. It wasn't a subject she was willing to discuss either. She had us call Henry "Dad" and that was that.

During our childhood, when we had any type of contact with Grandma Marie and Grandpa John, whether it was a visit or a letter, they never spoke to us about their son, our biological father. I believe Grandpa John and Grandma Marie were in an exceedingly difficult position. They had only one son, who had two daughters that he didn't have any contact with. He was an absent father. He hadn't ever met me and he hadn't seen Cherie since she was two years old. The only other contact he had with her was a ten minute phone call, when she was about 15 years old. Grandma Marie helped arrange it. I didn't have any knowledge of the phone call between Cherie and our father until recently, while I was finalizing the writing of this story.

It was particularly challenging on our paternal grandparents, and I don't blame them for any of our father's failures. They couldn't change or control him. Still, they lived with the heartache and shame of it all. I know it broke their hearts that he wasn't in our lives.

At twenty-two years old, I was married and had just had my first child. Being a parent for the first time and feeling the deep love you have for your own child, increased the recognition of the loss of my father. How could it be "OK" to not know your own child or be in their life? What was his story? I had always wondered about my biological father and decided that I would try and contact him through my paternal grandparents.

One evening at about 9 p.m. Pacific Time, I called my paternal grandparents' home in Florida and my Grandma Marie answered. She was surprised and happy to hear from me, as we had lost contact for a few years. She spoke about Grandpa John having passed away the previous year, 1980, which I hadn't known. She had thought someone in the family would have told me, but no one did and that upset her. I was sad to hear that he had passed and wondered how her life was now, without him. I told her that I would like to contact my father and she was very willing to give me his phone number. She also reminded me that they were three hours ahead of California, so it was midnight right now! Oops! Had I called my father at midnight, it would have really shocked him. We had a short visit; it was good to hear her voice, and we hung up promising to speak again very soon.

A few days later, I made the long-anticipated phone call to my biological father, David William McNamara. Hearing his voice for the first time filled me with emotions. I really didn't know how to feel. He was quiet and seemed deep in thought and guarded, speaking to his twenty-two-year-old biological daughter for the very first time. He was nervous, as was I, and from there, the conversations continued by phone over the next year and a half. He spoke many times about wanting to drive out from Florida, where he lived, to California to meet me. I learned about and spoke with his current wife and my half-sister, and he learned about my family, his first grandchild, and my childhood, including the abuse.

At times he would want to discuss his side of what happened between him and my mother, but I didn't really feel the need for that. It wasn't why I contacted him. I knew who my mother was, how she treated me, and what she had allowed to happen to me under her care. I understood him when he said he didn't love her. I wouldn't want anyone to stay married or together with someone they didn't love, not even for the children. No child wants to live in a house where the parents don't love or like each other and don't want to be together. The children can always tell if this is the case.

But in saying that, it is all about the children. You don't have to be married or living under the same roof to give your children the love and attention they need from both parents. He didn't do his part, he just went away and failed as a father for Cherie and me. I don't resent him; I really don't have any feelings either way for him. I am glad that we were able to get to know each other a little bit through our phone conversations.

He never drove out to meet me. He was a severely ill man who had cirrhosis of the liver and ended up in a hospital bed in the living room of his home for the last year or so of his life. He passed away about five years after I contacted him. He was fifty-eight years old when he died.

Once I made contact with my father, Grandma Marie sent me pictures of my father and other family members on the paternal side. After he passed away, I would learn from Grandma Marie that our father was an alcoholic. She said he would have been a very wealthy man, because he made a lot of money, but he had spent all his money on himself. She spoke openly and honestly about him.

I continued to have a relationship with Grandma Marie until she passed away from lung cancer on August 15, 1992. In the months prior to her passing, she sent me her wedding ring from her second marriage. She told me she wanted me to have it because I helped raise my younger brother and sister. That touched my heart, and I wear it daily on my right hand in remembrance of that period in our lives.

PART II

A CLOSER VIEW OF A PERPETRATOR AND AN ENABLER

Henry

CHAPTER 24

HENRY EDGAR MCINTIRE: STEPFATHER

Sadistic Child Molester and Abuser

Most people would be expecting a cruel and sadistic child molester to look like a monster, to have distinguishing features that would be a "red flag" or "the creepy guy lurking in the bushes," but there wasn't anything obvious about Henry that would make you think differently of him. He looked and acted basically normal to the outside world, and most people liked him. Child molesters and child abusers walk among us, as ordinary people, and we don't even know it. That's how they are able to easily gain access to children. It's crucial to understand this, or we won't ever end this horrific problem of child abuse.

I believe it is important to describe who Henry McIntire was in the world. What his personality traits were and what he physically looked like. How he interacted in his relationships, and how he generally lived his daily life. What was important to Henry? What did he value?

Henry was born on April 3, 1940, in the small town of Wynnewood, Oklahoma. He had two siblings that I knew of. I was told by a family member that Henry's father was an alcoholic and became extremely violent when he drank. The family would have to leave home quickly in order to get away from him. I also heard from another family member that his father died when Henry was about ten years old. He rarely spoke about his childhood, but when he did, he would speak of his core family being very poor, and that he didn't have much growing up. Henry had to work after school picking cotton in the fields to help support his family. He didn't appear to have had much of an education, but he did wear his high school class ring. I don't believe that he finished high school though.

At the time Cherie and I went to live with Henry, he would have been twenty-three years old. He was clean cut, tall, and had a slim muscular build with thinning black hair and blue eyes. He wore a glass eyeball in one of his eye sockets to replace his real eyeball that had to be removed following a childhood accident. I was told by a relative that he and some kids were playing with knives, and one landed in his eye. Eventually they couldn't save that damaged eye, and it had to be removed.

Henry was a completely different person in public than at home. People he worked with would speak about him as a "great guy." But at home we lived with Henry who was full of anger and rage. He would be evil, cruel, and sadistic, committing all forms of child abuse. At times he would also be physically abusive to Mom. Henry would go to the workplace or anywhere else and function normally, and people liked him. Then when he came home and was behind closed doors, he became quiet, cold, calculating, and short tempered. This temperament lasted until he was triggered. Then his anger would rise quickly, and he would react by physically assaulting the family member who triggered him. At times during these violent episodes, he would destroy items in the house. He would do it by knocking them over with a hard swing of his arms, or picking them up and throwing them, or kicking them. Eventually he would calm down and return to his quiet, cold, calculating, and short-tempered state of mind again. This behavior could happen once a day, every few days, or once a week; it was unpredictable.

As far as I knew, he wasn't confrontational to people outside of the home. He always kept that nice guy attitude. He taught us kids to never start a fight, but if a fight gets started and we are involved in it, we better finish it. Being the top dog was a way of life for him. At home he spoke like he was a badass, a tough guy who wasn't afraid of anybody or anything. Sometimes he would demonstrate how to fight or beat someone up, often using one of us kids to physically demonstrate what moves to use on them to win the fight. But I never saw him physically fight any "adult," and I never heard any stories about fights he was involved in.

I don't believe Henry was capable of having intimate relationships or of loving others. He never showed any true compassion or love toward anyone. Most of the time he didn't show any emotions, like he was disconnected from the world. He could be nice if he wanted something, or if it would benefit him. He knew how to play the game just long enough to reel people in and get what he wanted. I imagine that's how it was when he was dating each of his wives. I never saw him in a close loving relationship, not even with any of his biological children. He wasn't attentive or close to my younger brother and sister. He didn't show any concern, sadness, or compassion for others. Henry didn't have empathy for anyone. He would chuckle over someone else's sorrow.

Henry liked and owned different guns. He always had a loaded gun wrapped in a towel in the drawer of the nightstand, next to his side of the bed. Sometimes he would wear his holster and practice with his pistol in the living room at home. He would quickly pull the gun out of the holster and then put it back in, doing this over and over. Sometimes he would say, "Draw!" and quickly pull it out of the holster pointing it straight ahead, ready to shoot, like something you would see in a western movie. Other times he would twirl the gun on his first finger in the trigger area, before slipping it back into the holster. He would practice over and over, trying to perfect both of these tricks. Sometimes he would accidentally drop the pistol on the floor, and it would break one or more of the beautiful pearl grips on each side of the handle of the gun. Then he would make mom run down to the sporting goods store in town and buy new ones to replace the ones he broke. It could get expensive, but he didn't care. She would get angry that he was wasting money by being so careless, but she couldn't stop him.

Henry kept everything neat and clean. He was that way about himself personally, plus he took good care of the things that he owned. He would always say, "If you don't take care of what you have, you won't ever have anything." His vehicles were always clean. We kids had to wash and vacuum them on a regular basis. The yards of the houses where we lived were kept clean and neat. At a young age Henry taught us how to do yard work. We knew how to clean and groom a yard very well.

Henry watched a lot of television when he was home from work on nights and weekends. It is normally how he spent most of his time at home. He watched the news, some crime dramas, and a lot of old westerns. It was like he came from that era and could relate to them. I think he tried to resemble the tough guy through the way he dressed, his southern accent, and how he acted at home — tough and mean.

Henry worked at a variety of entry-level jobs over the years. He was a lot attendant at the car dealership in Illinois where my mother first met him, and his final employment was at one of the trailer factories in Hemet. He started out at the bottom, working as a sweeper, and moving himself up the ladder until he was in lower management. He worked at the trailer factory for many years, eventually retiring from there. The people he worked for loved him, and he had developed an extraordinarily strong work ethic. He was there every day and always on time. He was a quick and efficient employee. Any duty he took on, whether at work or home, he would do it well. I don't ever remember him calling in sick, except for the one time he had hernia surgery and wasn't able to work for a few weeks.

For fun, he liked to gamble at casinos or place bets at horse races. He enjoyed going to Las Vegas for the weekend, and we spent many long days at the different horse race tracks throughout Southern California. He also liked to go out on Friday or Saturday nights to the cocktail lounges in town, for alcoholic drinks and good food, like steak and lobster. Henry liked to dress well when he went out. He was pretty meticulous with his appearance, including his clothing. His cowboy boots had to be kept polished and buffed. That job was done by one of us kids, usually me.

If Henry were going out that night, he would be happy — kind of giddy — during the day, something that we never saw in him otherwise. He liked to listen to country music and go dancing, and sometimes he would even dance with other women at the bar. I'm sure that didn't go over very well with my mother. Grandpa said he would be flirtatious with the other women too.

There were times on a Saturday night where Henry would be playing cards with us kids (it wasn't normal for him to do this, it was a manipulative move on his part) while waiting for Mom to get tired and go to bed. They weren't going out that night. After she went to bed, he would play cards a bit longer with us, then he would have me go and check to see if Mom was asleep. If she was, he would have me sneak his cowboy boots out of the closet and bring them to him. He would put them on and out the door he would go, I'm guessing to the bar. The next day when Mom found out that he went out without her, she would question him about it. He would say that she was tired and fell asleep and then later on he decided that he wanted to go out to the bar for a bit. He did this a few times, and she would act like she believed him; I think she was trying to believe him. He had plans for something else that night, and it didn't involve her.

I don't believe he was faithful to my mother. I don't think that it was in his character to be faithful. Everything was about his needs and wants. If anything were to arise that might be in his benefit, he wouldn't think twice about it. It didn't matter who he hurt.

I never saw Henry have a problem with alcohol. If he drank at home, I never saw him get angry; he would actually loosen up a bit. He never drank very much or very often at home. It was usually a drink or two on the weekend, prior to going out. The heavier drinking happened outside of the house at the cocktail lounge or a bar. The knowledge I have of his violent behavior or abuse while drinking, is that he hit Mom on a couple different occasions while they were out partying. I never saw it myself, but I did see her bruises and she told me that Henry had hit her. I don't have any memory of him doing anything abusive to us kids while he was drinking alcohol. I never saw any illegal drugs or drug abuse by Henry either. To my knowledge, Henry was completely sober when he abused me or Cherie. Alcohol wasn't ever a piece of the puzzle.

There was only one time that I knew of during the time I lived with Henry, that he got in trouble with the law. He caused a car accident sometime in the seventies. He was driving and went into the other lane to pass a vehicle and hit another vehicle head on. The driver was injured and will probably limp for the rest of his life. It was a young guy, in a van, about nineteen years old. Henry had been drinking that night and was coming home from the bar with one other person in the car. Mom wasn't with him. Henry and his passenger were bruised and had lacerations, but otherwise were OK. He had to go to court over this and it made him extremely nervous. This is the only time in the years I lived with him that I saw him vulnerable and full of anxiety. He would speak to me about his concerns of what might happen to him, what his punishment might be. In the end he only got a minimal fine and life went on.

I don't know if Henry believed in God or had any kind of belief system. He never went to church with us, never spoke about his beliefs or God or any religion. After I moved out, I told one adult family member what Henry had done to us and they stated, "Oh, I always thought he was the good brother." They had no idea what had gone on all those years. Henry was able to hide this horrible sick side of himself, until I told my truth when he was thirty-five years old. Even then, he was still able to keep that part of himself hidden from the people he worked with, and other people who didn't want to believe the truth.

In the later years of Mom and Henry's life together, I was told that the tables had turned in their relationship. That Mom controlled how everything went, that Henry wasn't in charge anymore. I wonder what caused that change? Maybe she held the truth of who he really was over his head? Just a guess. Honestly, I can't even imagine that he wouldn't be in control. On the other hand, I can see her controlling everything, having it all her way if she could get away with it.

Henry never spent a day in jail for any of the criminal acts he committed on Cherie and me. I never saw or talked to him again after we met at the police station the day after my younger sister came to live with us. Henry wasn't ever held responsible for the child abuse and torture. I have always wondered if he ever abused any other children during his lifetime.

Mom remained married to Henry for the rest of his life. They were married for fifty years. Henry died September 13, 2014 at seventy-four years old. It is comforting to know that he doesn't walk the earth any longer, so he can't hurt anyone else.

My Biological Mother & me

CHAPTER 25
MOM-BIOLOGICAL MOTHER, ENABLER

After I moved in with my grandparents in 1974, I rarely had any contact with my mother except for the two different time periods when my younger siblings moved in with me. Eventually, it would become many, many years with no contact at all.

On April 4, 2008, when I was forty-nine years old, I received a phone call from my mother. I was shocked. She said she was calling because she wanted to connect with her three daughters... Hmm? Why now? She didn't have a relationship with any of us and hadn't talked to any of us in many, many years. She had chosen Henry over us a long time ago. Her voice sounded like an old woman's, and she thanked me for talking to her.

She was fortunate that I did speak with her that day. I owe her nothing and deep inside, she knows it. I told her, "Just because I am speaking to you it doesn't mean that I don't have many questions for you." She replied, "And I would be glad to answer them." Hmmm, I thought. Really? truthfully? Why now?

Mom wanted me to give Cherie and our younger sister her phone number and address, and I agreed to do this. Later, I would give each of my sisters her contact information, but neither were interested in having a relationship with her.

We made small talk for a few minutes about her health and my health and then we hung up. My mind was racing, and I was feeling overwhelmed and sick to my stomach.

A few days later I received a card in the mail from my mother. I have included images of the card for the readers review. I have blacked out my younger sister's name and my mother's phone number. I feel by sharing this card it gives the reader my mother's direct response.

Of all the ways that gratitude and thanks can be expressed...

First card from my mother after the phone call on April 4, 2008.

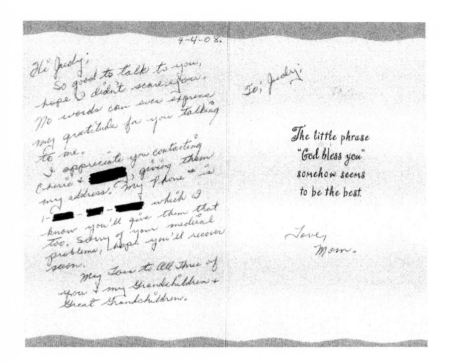

My birth name is "Judith," and I have gone by "Judith" or "Judi" since I was a teenager. I felt that "Judy" with a "y" was the young, abused girl who didn't have a voice, so I stopped using that name well over thirty years ago prior to the date of this card. It was a part of my healing process.

The statement Mom made in the card of "hope I didn't scare you" is a strange comment. She has met a few of the grandchildren but doesn't know them and hasn't had any contact with them for many, many years. She hasn't met any great-grandchildren, and this is how the parents want it to be.

Over a year later, I wrote to Mom asking the following questions that I have wanted to ask her all my life. The following is a copy of that letter, dated May 31, 2009. I whited out who it's written to because I had used her first name instead of Mom. Also, I blacked out my younger siblings' names for privacy. I now believe that Cherie was around ten years old or a little older when she told Mom, not nine years old.

May 31, 2009

When you called a year ago I told you that I had many questions for you. You stated that you would be glad to answer them.

Here is my first question:

Why didn't you protect Cherie and me from being raped by Henry? We were little children that he abused terribly. You would leave us in his care and he would beat me, then rape me tearing my insides creating unbearable pain and I would bleed and hurt terribly for days. This began at 6 years old for me and it happened over and over to me too many times to count. You had to know, there was blood in my underwear and you did the wash. Also I told you when I was 15 years old. I didn't tell you before because he had threatened me and I was scared to death of him. He had beaten me, broke my leg, stuck pins in my feet, made me eat cigarette butts, made me drink whiskey at 6 years old and many other sick and torturous things..........I remember it all. He has to live in fear for what he has done.

Cherie told you when she was about 9 years old, standing out in front of the Thrifty Drug Store while I waited in the car with ■■■ and ■■■. Henry then began raping me all of the time instead of the two of us.

We both suffered horrible abuse by Henry and you are still married to him today? Where was our Mother? Why did you choose him over us?

Write back don't call. I would like to know what your answer is.

Judi

Then after nine months she replied to me by sending this card

2/19/10

Dearest Judy;
I + Henry want to
send out apologies
to you. We are so
sorry and we are to
blame, not you.

You all were good
children, but we didn't
know how to handle
the situation, and took
it out on all of you. So Sorry
for our actions, we do
Love you all.
Sincerely,
Mom
&
Henry

I cried when I read her card. I felt a mixture of anger and sadness along with an overwhelming feeling that FINALLY, she had acknowledged that our childhood wasn't OK and that she and Henry are the reason. She even wrote it down on paper!

BUT, the card is a blanket apology. It didn't mention what

they were "so sorry" for. I won't even recognize the apology from Henry because there isn't one. You can't apologize for someone else, especially for something of this magnitude. The "y" in the signature "Henry," has an unusual curve to the tail.... exactly like Mom's written "y" that I have on the first card she sent me and throughout her writing. Did she sign it to look like he signed it? If so, that is sickening and more enabling. I can't imagine him signing it.

Mom wrote that "we are to blame, not you." I never thought I was to blame, and I haven't ever needed that clarification. Up to this point, Mom had blamed me and Ole Gram when relatives in Illinois inquired as to why I left home when I was sixteen years old, to move in with Grandma and Grandpa Byers. Per other relatives, she had told them that I was an out-of-control teenager on drugs and that my grandmother (her mother) was butting in and interfering with raising her children. She said that I didn't want to be disciplined, so I left and moved in with them. That was how Mom denied the reported violence and child abuse. Now everyone knows the TRUTH.

I can't emphasize enough how important it is to believe and support a child who says that they have been abused. It takes a lot for a child to come forward, and many never do. Some children like Cherie and me are being threatened by the abuser with severe violence if they tell. Plus, very often an adult is believed before a child. Believe the children, listen carefully and compassionately to what they are trying to tell you.

The statement "We didn't know how to handle the situation and took it out on all of you" is irrational! What was the situation? "Taking it out on all of you." What does this mean? Beating us? Breaking my leg? The torture? Mom being an enabler of this abuse? Is the sexual abuse included in this? What explanation could Mom give about her husband raping her two young daughters repeatedly? What "situation" would warrant this behavior? I'll never understand her. She chose him over her beautiful daughters. She remained married to Henry and lived with him until he died. How easy it is to just send this card and say, "so sorry."

I never wrote back. There just wasn't a reason to. I had been looking for answers that I'm never going to get. I never had and never will have a normal relationship with my biological mother. I let it go and freed myself that day. I was blessed with my Ole Gram from the day I was born. She has always been my mother.

PART III

WHAT IT LOOKS LIKE TO BE A SURVIVOR

CHAPTER 26
CHERIE'S THOUGHTS AND WORDS

~Written by Cherie~

Sixty-Seven Years Old

*T*oday, I'm reflecting on my life and putting all of this into perspective. It is important for my voice to be a part of this book. In my childhood I was a very scared little girl. I was just trying to get through each day by going along to keep the peace at any price, blocking out all the horrific ongoing abuse. I was trying to make my childhood seem as normal as possible in my mind. I also strived to keep myself removed from the situation; it was my coping mechanism.

I began dating when I was sixteen years old. I quickly ended up in an abusive relationship, and after I became an adult we got married. I didn't have a strong model of a healthy relationship in my life. I chose what I knew, the relationship that influenced my life daily: Mom and Henry's relationship. I also suffered from low self-esteem and low self-

worth, so at the time I didn't have the strength to rise above it for my own well-being. After my daughter was born, I knew I had to leave this relationship because it wasn't healthy for either one of us. I got a divorce.

As an adult, I was afraid to be alone and I wasn't at peace. I quickly connected into another unhealthy relationship and marriage. I had not had any counseling or anything to help me heal or improve the relationship choices I was making. The second marriage was failing, so after thirteen years I got a divorce.

Shortly after leaving my relationship, I met the man who I would go on to have a son with. Our son was born in 1994. This was a completely different relationship than what I usually chose. It began with a friendship, and we had many things in common. We both came from broken families and had a history of abuse in our childhood that neither of us had gotten help with. In 1997, we made it official and got married and continued raising our son together.

In 2004, I joined Judi in joint counseling. As the counseling progressed, I was able to come to terms with what I had lived through in my childhood, and its effects on my adult life and well-being. I had to learn to forgive myself, love myself, and lose the victim mentality to heal. I had to accept what happened, instead of blocking it out. I came through a very dark, foggy tunnel into the light and saw what peace and joy in life can bring. It helped me to break through the robotic existence I was living and become free. I continued in joint counseling with Judi for about eighteen months, until I moved to Texas, in February 2006.

A few years later I went back into counseling as I was still struggling with the awareness of who I was. I didn't know how to have my needs met, or how to feel loved. I was still experiencing low self-esteem and struggling with self-love. The counseling helped me to become more aware of who I was, and to become more in tune with my mind, body, and soul. But there are still times where I struggle with anxiety, depression, and PTSD (post-traumatic stress disorder) from childhood trauma.

We continued raising our son together until he was an adult. I then came to the realization that the relationship had to end for both of us to be able to live healthy lives. In 2015, I divorced my son's father. I moved to another city to start my new single life. This is where I met and married my current husband, in 2020. I feel more loved and cared for in this relationship than I ever have in my life. I now feel free, happy in my own skin, and at peace.

I realize how precious life is and try to enjoy every moment with as positive an outlook as possible. I have always felt unconditionally loved and taken care of by God. I want to leave every person or place better than I found them. I strive to love my family unconditionally, accepting each one where they are, for the person they are on their path in life. I accept my truth and I am proud of my survival. I do all I can to live my life's purpose.

I am a wife, mom, nana, stepmom and sister. I have wonderful children and grandchildren. I am a retired Registered Nurse, after forty-three years of nursing. I spent the last fourteen years of my career working in Hospice Care.

Today I am a determined, courageous, and wise woman who is coming to terms with my childhood and my adult life. Through the highs and the lows of life, I own my decisions, right or wrong; love myself first; and accept who I am. All is well with my soul.

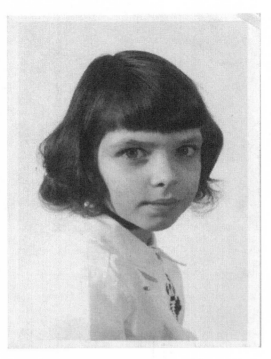

Cherie seven years old

One day when we were in joint counseling together, when we were both in our mid-forties, Cherie tearfully mentioned that she had found this picture of herself, from before she went to California to live, before anything happened to her. She said, "I see this little girl and I think that was me! That little girl. I wonder how she would have turned out, had all of this not happened...I feel sorry for that little girl."

It was heartbreaking to hear Cherie articulate that tragedy. The tragedy of our lives and so many others' lives. I wonder how all the abused children of the world would have turned out if we could have stopped the abuse from ever happening in the first place.

CHAPTER 27

LIVING AS A SURVIVOR OF CHILD ABUSE

Sixty-Four Years Old

As I come to the end of sharing my story, I feel a sense of peace. I have weathered the storm, but I'll never forget where I have been, not the pain or the suffering, it can't be wasted. I don't carry the weight of being a victim, I have immense gratitude for being a strong survivor.

Before I wrote this book, no one knew the entire story. There was too much to tell, and much of it was too difficult to talk about. It was a story that had been misconstrued, and some would have liked it to be buried and never spoken about. Everyone will now have the opportunity to know the truth. Gram and Grandpa Byers deserved the truth to be told. They should be honored and remembered for their tireless devotion to help their granddaughters.

I believe in forgiveness, but truthfully I haven't forgiven Mom or Henry. I don't feel it in my heart. I have been told that forgiveness is for me, not them, but I still can't get there. Henry died without taking any responsibility for his horrific criminal acts. My Mother is still alive today and doesn't acknowledged the depth of her actions, or inactions. How do you forgive someone who has caused so much suffering and pain, but exhibits no remorse? I have accepted the past, there isn't anything I can do to change what happened. However, I can change the future by shining a light on the crime of child abuse.

When I got married the second time, I married the man I dreamed of in my childhood. We have now been married for thirty wonderful years. Steve is loving, kind, patient, and compassionate. He is my best friend and I have complete trust in him. He has helped to free me from my past. I have shared the darkest moments of my childhood with him, and always received his love and compassion in return. I also have a loving relationship with Steve's family.

We raised our four children together, and then Steve adopted my two children from my first marriage when they were adults. They all love him dearly. We have grandchildren and great-grandchildren, who all bring love, joy and happiness to our lives. Our wealth is our family, and we have been blessed in that area.

Steve also became more involved in the writing of this book than I ever expected. On a regular basis, I would read him my newly written chapter, and he would give his feedback on the content. Steve compassionately listened to story after story with shock and disbelief that someone could do this to a child. It validated the importance of writing this book and was also a reflection of the world we live in. In my world this happened, and in his world it didn't. Our relationship has been a strong support that has helped me find the courage to write this book.

It is my life's purpose to share our story of abuse and survival with the world. If we remain silent, perpetrators can get away with child abuse and continue to abuse others. Instead, I will use my knowledge, compassion, and understanding to help heal both myself and others. My deepest wish is by sharing our story, it will save other children from being abused. I also hope to empower victims of child abuse by motivating them to use all of the healing resources available today, so they can rise above these horrific criminal acts and live the life that they would choose.

At my core I am a gentle person who likes the simple things in life. I enjoy spending time with my family and friends, that's where my heart is. I love to laugh, especially with children because it is so deep and honest. I am a peacemaker. I love all animals, just watching them brings me joy. I am intuitive and connected to the world and those around me. I can easily feel the pain of other people. It's very important for me to feel free. I am grateful that I can deeply feel love, experience joy, and have compassion for others. I see so much good and beauty in the world.

At sixty-four years old, I have joy and peace in my life. I have the support of both family and friends. They are a huge blessing. It's my happy ending. I know that I could have easily ended up on many other horrific paths. I don't take my life for granted. I am extremely grateful for all the love and grace I have received along the way. The older I get, the more I stand in awe and gratitude for what Grandpa and Gram gave of themselves to help me.

Judi holding "The Muff," September 18, 2020

In Chapter 1, "Where My Life Began," I spoke about "the muff" and how as a child I loved playing with it when I lived on the farm. Well, I was surprised when I received a special gift in the mail from my Aunt Merikay in June of 2019. It was the original muff! And the hat that went with it. She and my Uncle Butch had come out to visit us in May of 2019. During the visit, she had read the first chapter of my book and she saw what I had written in that chapter about how we had enjoyed playing with the muff when we were little girls living on the farm. She didn't say a word to me about it, but a few weeks after she had returned home I received a box in the mail and there was the muff, along with a beautiful letter. Aunt Merikay still had it after moving across the United States twice, and fifty-eight years later. In her letter she wrote, "Surprise! Enjoy a part of your happy memories Honey! I now know why I couldn't get rid of this; God had a perfect plan and a perfect place for my Muff.

CHAPTER 28
OLE GRAM
Madge Teresa Defenbaugh-Byers
Maternal Grandmother/Mother

I am writing this chapter about my maternal grandmother because I want to honor the beautiful person she was and emphasize the impact she had on my life. Her influence was immeasurable. Gram was a loving role model who translated into resilience for me. She demonstrated how someone can reach into the heart and mind of a child who had been abused and make a difference. She changed the course of my life.

Gram grew up as an only child. Her mother had a chronic illness that left her lying in bed or on the couch most of Gram's life. Because of this, her father let her bring her Shetland pony into their home so she could share and enjoy it with her mother. Gram had a love of horses, like her father. She spent a lot of her time at the home of her aunt and uncle and their children, since her father needed to work, and her mother was so ill. In 1927, a few months before Gram gave birth to her first child, her mother passed away. Gram was in her early twenties when this happened.

She was married to her loving husband Theodore Driscoll Byers, or Grandpa Byers, in 1926 and had three children with him. Their first child was a son, named Richard; their second child was a daughter, my mother; and Merikay was their youngest daughter and child. The children were born seven years apart. Gram said this gave her time with each child when they were very young, because the other children were old enough to go to school. Gram and Grandpa Byers had been married for fifty years when he died in 1976.

Gram was naturally a nurturer, very loving, kind, and compassionate, plus she was intelligent and funny. She loved children and as she would say, "They are the most important; after all, they didn't ask to be born."Gram taught us that we all need to help children to be their best, and for us to be patient and kind, understanding that they are children. She used her words to teach or discipline. She never used physical force.

She was a great teacher of life and found a good balance between work and playtime. She was fun, with a wonderful smile and laugh. She was always planning things for us to see and do. Everyone—family and friends—loved Gram. She had a special way of making you feel important. It was the best day for her when all of us were together. She enjoyed the simple things in life, good food, family, and friends.

Gram was a skilled gardener of both vegetables and flowers. When I moved in with her, we spent fun times out in the yard gardening together. Even when she lived in the mobile home park and only had a small area to plant her vegetables, she used that land resourcefully and grew a variety of vegetables including delicious potatoes, tomatoes, and bell peppers. Gram believed that you must always plant your potatoes on Good Friday in order to get a good crop. Many years ago in Illinois, during a storm on Good Friday, she had Uncle Butch outside helping her plant the potatoes while the wind was blowing and it was raining. She wasn't going to miss the perfect potato planting day! Uncle Butch loved her like a mother. I learned a lot from her and still enjoy growing beautiful plants and flowers today.

She also enjoyed cooking and baking. Our family were the lucky recipients of her food. Most of her cooking and baking was from scratch. She would add a little of this and a cup of that, and it all turned out perfect and delicious! She lived during the Depression, and it taught her to not waste anything. She could be very creative with what food she had in the house, including leftovers. I also love to bake, especially with my grandchildren. The inspiration came from her.

Gram read the daily newspaper in the evening, after everything was done, and it was quiet in the house. She was a night person, and it was relaxing for her. The next day she would share what was going on out in the world with me. She liked to learn about all the new things. Gram stressed the importance of education and knowledge. She was a woman who was ahead of her time.

She had a sweet tooth and enjoyed a fresh piece of cake or a homemade cookie. Her cookie drawer was kept stocked so that when the grandchildren came over they knew right where they could find a "treat." She would say, "What good am I if I don't have something to offer them when they come over to visit?" She knew it brought them joy, and in return it brought her great joy.

Gram felt sleep was a waste of time! Of course, we all need sleep, and many times I would find her sleeping upright, in her chair! One time when she was staying at our home over the Christmas holiday, she went into my son's bedroom to look out the window to watch my children riding their new bicycles outside. She was gone for quite a while, so I went looking for her and found her stretched out asleep on my son's bed! She was such a character!

She was faithfully late to everything; it was something that the family lovingly teased her about. The family would tell her to be there a half-hour earlier than the expected time to try to make it all work out, but she soon caught on to what they were doing!

Gram was a physically small person, but always bought a large car. She would say that it was important to buy a large car just in case you got into an accident, then you would have protection between you and the other vehicle. She had a 1963 Buick Electra that she and Grandpa purchased brand new off the storeroom floor in Illinois. It was light green with a white interior. When she drove this car she could barely see over the steering wheel. When they sold the farm in Illinois and moved to California, Gram and Great-Aunt Margaret, Grandpa's sister, took turns driving it out here. It was loaded with their personal belongings packed all around Grandpa, who made the trip riding in the backseat. Gram called the car "Old Betsy," and she didn't want to leave this good car behind. There was rust damage on the lower sides of the car because of the highway salt in Illinois.

Old Betsy was the car I learned how to drive in after I moved in with Gram and Grandpa. Gram would take me out to the rural areas in south Hemet so we could trade seats, putting me behind the wheel. She would calmly direct me what to do, and down the road we would go. Gram loved the freedom that driving gave her. It was one of her favorite things. Old Betsy would end up being my first car when I was eighteen. She bought herself another large car, an Oldsmobile Delta 98. Just like with Old Betsy, she could barely see over the new steering wheel. It was cute to see her driving around town in that big car.

Gram was selfless, always putting her family first. She would say to me, "I'm an old woman and I have lived my life. I don't need new things, you need a new dress, you are young and beautiful." She didn't have a lot of money, but always gave what she had to make my life better.

Since I was a child, I believed that Gram was an angel and that I was the luckiest granddaughter in the world to be able to call her "my" Grandmother, but for me she was always my mother. She and Grandpa gave me a safe place in this world. During the horrible years of suffering through child abuse and neglect, I held on to the memories that I had from when I lived on the farm. Knowing there was someone out there who loved me gave me hope for a better life and kept me going.

One day Aunt Merikay got a call from the manager of the mobile home park where Ole Gram lived. She said that Gram hadn't opened her drapes that day, and there weren't any signs of anyone being home, but her car was in the driveway. My cousin Gretchen went over to check on her and found her lying on her bed. She had passed away. Her death appeared as gentle as the way she treated everyone in life. She had sat down on her bed, still in her daytime clothing, and then laid over, with the upper half of her body resting on her bed. She looked so peaceful. It was a gift that she was able to stay in her home until the end. It was always her wish. I believe she was granted that wish because she gave so much to everyone else in her life. It was a gift to me also.

With honor,
I dedicate this book to our maternal grandmother,
"Ole Gram."

(Judi, 18 years old; Gram 70 years old, and Cherie, 20 years old)

She guided and cared for Cherie and me throughout our lives. Her
strength of character, unconditional love, and tireless devotion was
the driving force for the betterment of both my life and Cherie's life.
She changed the course of our lives.

TOOLS FOR HEALING AND EMPOWERMENT

I want to share what has helped me to take back my life, living beyond the child abuse and trauma, to find peace.

Counseling: Consider professional counseling. Some people will benefit from individual counseling and others might find that group counseling works out the best for them. Every person works through things differently. If you do choose counseling, be picky; therapists have specialties and use several types of therapy. Find a professional therapist who is knowledgeable in child abuse and trauma and has the therapeutic courage to open up the subjects victims tend to avoid. Keep looking until you find the right therapist for you, one you can connect with and learn from. You need to both trust your therapist and like your therapist. There are places that offer counseling at no cost to the victim.

Go to counseling for as long as you need to. You will gain a better understanding about child abuse and trauma and how it has affected your life. There are tools that you can learn to use to help you live better. You will be validated that what happened to you wasn't your fault. You will find the safety and freedom to be yourself and speak your truth. It will be a safe place for you to go and share your pain and sorrow. You will learn about your triggers and how to cope effectively with them. Be good to yourself by allowing the gift of counseling. You will know when it's time for counseling to end, but do return to counseling as often as you need to. Checking back in with your counselor can help you to continue to stay on track and live a better life.

Write about what happened to you: Writing this book has been an incredibly healing journey. Whether you journal for yourself or write a book, it will help you bring buried memories to the surface so that you can work through them. It will promote healing and well-being. In my adult life I do think about the child abuse and trauma; it never leaves you. But I hadn't thought about it as intensely as what was required for writing this book. I knew it would be difficult to spend so much time thinking about the abuse that I experienced as a child, but I didn't realize the extent of healing it would also provide.

In counseling I learned that for my well-being and healing, I must set a place at the table for everything that has happened to me in my life. Everything needs to be up on-board. You can't fix anything that you haven't acknowledged is broken. To write the book, it was necessary for me to revisit the memories of abuse at a deeper level so I could gather all the facts and put them into words. At times memories that had been suppressed would also come forward. Writing this book was an excellent way to follow my counselor's guidance. It has been a cathartic experience for me.

Support groups: Spending time with others who have suffered through child abuse and/or trauma will greatly benefit you. You will bond with these people. They are your "tribe." You speak the same language others don't understand.

Choose healthy relationships: Abusive relationships can happen in many areas of your life. This includes your employer, coworkers, spouse, friends, family members, and children. It doesn't matter who they are or what your relationship with them is; it isn't OK or healthy for anyone to abuse you. I no longer wish to associate with people who are not good for my mental health.

My mother and my stepfather ruined my childhood, and I wasn't going to let them ruin my adult life. After I left home at sixteen years old, they continued with their lives as though nothing happened, and they had not done anything wrong. As far as I know, they didn't go to counseling to get the help they needed. For me to be healthy — physically, mentally, and emotionally — I would choose to not have them in my adult life. Surround yourself with healthy, happy people.

Read non-fiction books/literature and watch movies/ series about child abuse and trauma that offer education on the subject, plus show resilience and triumph: Early on when I started the healing journey, I found such connection when I would watch or read something about child abuse. At first it was too difficult for me, so I didn't. But once I made the decision to try and honor what other victims of child abuse had been through by reading or watching their story, it significantly helped me. I would cry and cry, feeling so many different emotions. But I also felt validated by what the survivors were expressing. I also read two excellent books on trauma. I can't express enough how informative it was for me. I now have a greater understanding of myself, and my siblings. Questions I have pondered most of my life were answered in these books. Why I behave, think and act in certain ways, and then the same about my siblings. I learned how child neglect and abuse can have a direct effect on brain development. It can change how we respond to the world, how we love, and how we connect with others. I have listed these books on trauma in the back of this book under "Information and Resources on Child Abuse and Trauma."I also read books written by child abuse survivors. At times, these stories helped to bring up memories I had suppressed. I read about amazing people who survived the unthinkable, coming out of a terrible situation with so much good to give to the world. These stories continue to be valuable to me and I still cry a lot and feel a connection to the survivors.

When beneficial, speak openly about your truth: In the year before my cousin Cynde's unexpected death in November of 2015, she sent me a text with the following saying. *"Your story could be the key that unlocks someone else's prison. Don't be afraid to share it."* She knew I was working on writing a book about my abusive childhood, but she also knew that I struggled with having to relieve the pain and trauma as I wrote the book. It is a beautiful reminder that we could take something that was so damaging to us and find the good in it—by sharing it with others. The common thread can be so powerful. Helping someone else always leaves me with the best feeling.

Don't connect gender to your abuse: The gender of the abuser isn't the reason they abused you. This was a mentally ill or very traumatized/damaged individual. Don't let it change or affect your relationships with a person of the same gender as your abuser. Throughout my life I have spoken to many people who have been through several types of abuse. I have noticed that the gender of the abuser can become a negative to the abused person. For instance, a female who was abused by a male either has a challenging time having a relationship with males, or they speak negatively about males. Their gender isn't the reason that they abused anyone. This can be the domino effect of the child abuse and trauma, going beyond the abused person, continuing to damage others. Because of this bias, I see many people miss out on wonderful healthy relationships. If you feel this way about a gender, you can get help to work through this in counseling.

Embrace who you are: The abuse and trauma I was subjected to as a child changed my life forever. Instead of resisting it, I am learning to embrace it. It is who I am. By embracing what triggers me, and surrendering to the emotion or feeling, I am letting go, and letting it pass through me. As time goes by, I'm learning to find a way to be OK with it all. I must be my authentic self. I'm not a victim, I am a strong survivor of child abuse and trauma.

My counselor explained that the idea that we normally have in our mind of "getting over it" is sort of an illusion, you never get over it. What you do is learn to accommodate to it. You learn to have it not be a debilitating force.

Turn the awful experience around and find the good that can come out of it: Let it be the catalyst. We must look for the positive in everything. Sometimes you can learn what to do, from what not to do. The experience helped me to be a better mother and grandmother. I learned how powerful love is. I enjoy the simple things in life because I didn't have them when I was young. What I suffered as a child motivated me to write this book to help others who have suffered through child abuse, and to bring awareness in order to prevent child abuse.

Use your empathy to help others: Removing my younger brother and sister from the care of my mother and stepfather and raising them in my home was very healing for me. To be able to help them at that time in my life helped me to regain my self-worth. I can rise above the abuse to help others who have more difficulty in rising. I am able and willing to share my experience with others who have gone through child abuse to offer understanding and compassion.

Spirituality: Searching out the meaning of life and having my faith has helped me to find peace.

Self-Care: Take good care of yourself, no one can do it as well as you can. No one will ever know the extent of everything you have gone through and at what level you suffer silently today. Do everything that you can do to bring wellness and joy into your life. Love yourself.

INFORMATION ON CHILD ABUSE & TRAUMA

Websites:

Childhelp
https://www.childhelp.org

American Society for the Positive Care of Children
http://americanspcc.org

Hope for Children Foundation
http://hopeforchildrenfoundation.org

Dave Pelzer: http://www.davepelzer.com

CDC-Fast Facts: Preventing Child Abuse & Neglect
https://www.cdc.gov/violenceprevention/
childabuseandneglect/fastfact.html

Books:

The Body Keeps the Score: Brain, Mind, and Body in the Healing of Trauma
Bessel Van Der Kolk, M.D.

A Child Called "It"
Dave Pelzer

Spilled Milk
K.L. Randis

Etched in Sand
Regina Calcaterra

Girl Unbroken
Regina and Rosie Maloney

What Happened to You? Conversations on Trauma, Resilience, and Healing
Bruce D. Perry, M.D., PhD, and Oprah Winfrey

If You Tell: A True Story of Murder, Family Secrets, and the Unbreakable Bond of Sisterhood
Gregg Olsen

Why Me?
Sarah Burleton

The Family Next Door
John Glatt

Shattered Silence: the Untold Story of a Serial Killer's Daughter
Melissa G. Moore

Movies:

Mystic River: 2003
Directed by Clint Eastwood

Spotlight: 2015
Directed by Tom Mc Carthy

Documentaries and Series:

The Trials of Gabriel Fernandez
Netflix, six-part documentary series, 2020

Children of the Underground
FX, five-episode documentary series 2022

Surviving Jeffrey Epstein
Lifetime, four episodes, 2020

Leaving Neverland
HBO documentary, 2-part series, 2019
Director: Dan Reed

After Neverland
Oprah Winfrey hosts a conversation featuring Wade Robson
and James Safechuck, alongside *Leaving Neverland* director Dan
Reed, before an audience of sexual abuse survivors and others
whose lives have been impacted by it.

Television shows:

The Oprah Winfrey Show
Includes numerous impactful episodes covering child abuse.
The OWN Network

Music:

(self-titled)
CD or album:
By Marcus Mumford

CHILD ABUSE HOTLINE

TO SEEK HELP

OR

REPORT CHILD ABUSE:

Childhelp National Child Abuse Hotline:

1-800-4-A-CHILD

(1-800-422-4453)

Or

childhelphotline.org

Available 24 hours a day, 7 days a week

Childhelp has extensive resources to offer assistance. Call or check out their website.

A report of child abuse is made every ten seconds in the United States.

Every year, more than 4 million referrals are made to child protection agencies involving more than 4.3 million children (a referral can include multiple children).

The United States has one of the worst records among industrialized nations – losing on average 5 children every day to child abuse and neglect.

In 2019 alone, state agencies found over 656,000 victims of child maltreatment, but that only tells part of the story.

This would pack 10 modern football stadiums.

(Information from https://www.childhelp.org 6/2023)

In loving memory of my cousin Cynde

Beginning in childhood, Cynde and I shared a close bond and a common thread that would continue throughout our lives until her unexpected and tragic death in the fall of 2015.

The sunflowers on the cover of this book and throughout the book are in memory of Cynde. She loved sunflowers and grew some of the most beautiful ones I have ever seen. I miss you and love you Cynde.

My loyal support dog, Petey. Always lying next to me day after day as I wrote this book. Petey crossed over the Rainbow Bridge on June 14, 2022.

ACKNOWLEDGEMENTS

Throughout the years while writing my book, family and friends would often ask how it was coming along, offering encouragement and interest in reading it one day. I always felt the love and support from each one of you. I hope you know how important those kind words were, they helped me to continue writing. There are too many names to mention, so please know that I am honoring you right here. Much love to all of you.

To those who read the different versions of the manuscript as it evolved, I am grateful for your willingness, time, and patience. I know this is a difficult story to read. The suggestions or insight from each of you were a guiding light along the way. Amy, Alice, Aunt Merikay, Cherie, Holli, Ivan, John, Lenae, and Vanessa.

My sister Cherie, your willingness to be vulnerable, the courage to share your truth, and the strength it took to get back into the darkness of your memories is so honorable. I'm proud of you. I will always be grateful for your encouragement and help to tell OUR important story.

Aunt Merikay and Uncle Butch, thank you for always standing with us in the truth of our childhood. No words can express what this has meant, or how it has helped us to heal. Thank you for your continual loving support.

John, thank you for your lifelong dedication to helping trauma and child abuse victims. You have guided us to find healing and peace in our lives. In doing so you have changed the world for the better. I am forever grateful for all the help you have given me, my family and my friends.

Vanessa, you came into my life at the perfect time. Thank you for lifting me up with your words of encouragement and validation. The time we spent discussing the manuscript was a gift to me. Your bright light and knowledgeable guidance will help so many find their way.

Scott, thank you for your time, guidance, and kindness. I am truly grateful.

Alice, I was touched that you were glad I told my true story because you thought it might help someone. Your words were a validation for me. Thank You!

My granddaughter Haley, thank you for your interest and artistic ideas for the cover design of the book.

Grandma Marie, your hobby of photography might have ended when your models (Cherie and Judy) left Illinois, but over sixty years later they have helped to bring this story to life. Thank you!

My stepdaughter Amy, I am so grateful for your interest and support of my book, and for your loving heartfelt note. It left me with a strong sense of peace. It's also quite insightful of you to note, "I had the last word!"

My grandson Ivan, I won't ever forget our long discussion the day you read my manuscript. You are truly beyond your years. Thank you for your genuine interest and love.

My friend Deb, thank you for sending me the wonderful books on writing, very thoughtful of you. I appreciate your loving support and positive encouragement.

My daughter-in-law Lenae, thank you for having an interest in my book and reading it. I appreciate all of your kind words and your continual love and support.

My son Clint, thank you for your encouraging words and loving support through the years while I was writing my book. I truly needed to hear them, especially from you.

Brent and Shelly, I am grateful that you read my book, and are supportive of me sharing this story. Thank you for your love and compassion.

To my editor Laurie Chittenden, I am grateful to have found you. From the very beginning you had compassion for this subject and understood the importance of sharing this story. Your insight and professional skills are exceptional. Thank you for helping me to share my truth with the world.

To my copy editor Brooks Becker, thank you for your skilled and detailed focus on the manuscript. I am honored that you felt this was a meaningful book and am happy that you worked on it.

Mandi Lynn of Stone Ridge Books, thank you for all of your hard work to format the book and create the remarkable cover design. I admire how you artistically captured the essence and tone of this story.

My dog Petey, thank you for being my sweet companion, laying right next to me, day after day, through the years, tears, and struggles, as I strived to retrieve these stories buried deep inside of me. I always felt your love.

My daughter Holli, thank you for your love and unwavering support. You have always listened while I shared my childhood stories with interest and compassion; it touches my heart. Thank you for reading the final manuscript and sharing detailed insights during a very difficult time in your life. I am honored by your grace.

My husband Steve, thank you for understanding how important writing this book would be for me on my journey of healing. You have shown me endless love and support in every aspect of writing and publishing this story. I am forever grateful. You are the Love of my Life.

My cousin Cynde, thank you for continuously encouraging me to share my story. I'll never forget the final words you spoke to me on the last day we spent time together on earth, "Now you finish that book! You finish that book!"

The Divine guidance I have received throughout my life, has brought me through it all. I live from a place of gratitude.

Cherie 60 years old and Judi 57 years old, Yellowstone National Park

I have not written my story,
To wallow in the pain

Only to bring it to the light,
So it wasn't in vain

Please consider passing your copy of this book on to someone else who might like to read it. Maybe with more awareness in the world, we can end child abuse one day.

You can contact the author

Judi A. Schwab

at:

jaschwab@outlook.com

Made in the USA
Columbia, SC
11 November 2024

45880647R00159